# MONTESSORI FOR FAMILY AND COMMUNITY

Susan Mayclin Stephenson

II

## CONTENTS

Introduction . . . 1

Birth to Three Years . . . 10

Age Three to Six Years . . . 39

My Primary and Elementary Consultant and Mentors . . . 74

Age Six to Twelve Years . . . 81

Age Twelve to Eighteen Years . . . 115

Conclusion . . . 139

Maria Montessori . . . 140

Other Books in This Series . . . 147

# INTRODUCTION

In the fall of 2018, I was in Iasi, Romania to celebrate the translation of *The Joyful Child: Montessori, Global Wisdom for Birth to Three.* Following a presentation of the book to parents and teachers, Catalin Ivan—Romanian representative to the European Parliament, and member of The Committee on Culture and Education—suggested that some of these ideas, such as mixed age grouping in classrooms and the value of working together at home and school—might be helpful for his constituents as there are many villages with too few children to warrant the creation of a school. I agreed with this observation, remembering that Dr. Montessori said in the conclusion of her book *The Discovery of the Child*:

> *What an immense advantage belongs to this method, one which would make very easy the instruction in rural schools and in schools in small villages in the provinces, in which there are a few children, and in which many different classes with many teachers could not be formed. The result of our experiment is that a single [teacher] can handle children who are at such varying levels.*

A few years earlier I had been interviewed on television in Ramallah, a city in the Middle East. At the end of the interview a Palestinian father present in the studio said that the Montessori ideas I was sharing were examples of their family values and aligned with the ways in which children had been educated for centuries, working together and caring for each other.

In a boarding school in Nepal, I met poor children who lived in small villages where there were no schools, having traveled ". . . one day by bus, five days walking" to get to Kathmandu for an education. Because of lack of funds, the students oversaw many aspects of running the school, such as cleaning and doing laundry and taking care of each other. The teachers were pleased to know that such responsibilities are valued as an important part of the curriculum in Montessori schools.

There are many aspects of Montessori philosophy and practice valued by educators in many countries around the world, representing a great variety of cultures. Here are a few of the main points. In the following chapters I will share details of how they are adapted to meet the needs of children of different ages:

*Natural age grouping as found in family and community*

Montessori is based on strengthening the connection within the family and the community from the first days of life through high school. As adults we know that our friends are usually not the same age as we are. We are friends and colleagues because of shared interests and responsibilities, and because we enjoy working and spending time together.

It is the same in a Montessori class. The friendships formed are based on interests, older children working with, helping, teaching, and learning from the younger; the reverse is also true as the younger often help older children. The specific age-grouping in Montessori schools is not arbitrary but based on many years of observation. Children and young adults learn differently and have different needs at different ages or stages of development. The age groupings are birth to age one; 1-3 years; 3-6 years; 6-12 years; and 12-18 years.

*Mastery of everyday life skills*

The daily life of a specific culture is reflected in activities known as *practical life work* in a Montessori class. Here a child learns how to care for himself, others, and the environment. He has already observed cooking, eating, cleaning, gardening, helping each other, and so much more, in the home since birth. In the first Montessori class in Italy, as soon as the children were allowed to participate in this real work, they left the toys behind and never played with them again. This preference came from the children and was a surprise to the adults.

Mastery of these practical skills is the goal in all levels of Montessori education. They fulfill many needs. For example, they prepare a person to participate in and to contribute to, the daily life of family, community, and school. They provide practical challenges to continually improve a skill. They give a feeling of value and importance to the child because the work is valuable. And they provide opportunities to help others, a situation that brings happiness.

How does focusing on the work of the daily life of the family and community have such power for good? We know this from experience, but now the question is being researched by neuroscientists. What we are learning is this kind of daily real work supports the development of *executive functions* in the brain. Here is that one list of executive functions that are continually improved: observation, focus, self-control and monitoring, flexible thinking, working memory, time-management, defining and achieving goals, and stress tolerance. Children and young adults experiencing this kind of living and learning tend to change, to become happier, kinder, and life-long learners.

> *The teacher* [and parent] *must know and experience in her daily life the secret of childhood. Through this she arrives not only at a deeper knowledge, but at a new kind of love which does not become attached to the individual person.... And this revelation transforms her also. It is a thing that touches the heart, and little by little it changes people.*
>
> —Montessori, *The Absorbent Mind*

*Nature*

Spending time in nature and learning to observe and care for plants and animals and each other, provide experiences—outside or in the home and classroom—that improve physical, mental, and emotional health. Exposure to the changing seasons teaches not only the related academics of geography and science and appreciation of nature's beauty but it teaches that there are also seasons in a person's life. The goal of Montessori at all ages is for the individual to learn to create a balance in life that one sees in the world of nature, with time for working, interacting with others, and time to process experiences, to rest, and to think.

*Local culture*

Just as with the everyday practical work of the local culture, other areas of culture are explored through special well-thought lessons and activities—art, music, dance, celebrations, sports, and more. And along with learning about one's own culture, life skills and interests from cultures around the world are presented and explored.

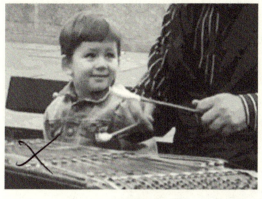

An awareness of life in a child's family and culture begins at birth. And as you will see later, a lot of valuable learning occurs in the early days and months and years. In the Montessori preschool class there are special ways of experiencing, and mastering, the work and culture a child has been observing. Through hands-on activities in the classroom, he will learn about physics, biology, the arts and sciences, and history and geography. At ages 6-18 the exploration of these subjects become more academic, but they will always reflect each student's interests and specific skills so that the learning is enjoyed and retained.

*Enjoying academics:*

When I was in school, studying because it was required, or cramming for a test to get a good grade, I remembered very little of the materials covered. This is not the situation in Montessori where there are no grades and a minimum of requirements. For ages 6-18, the basic requirements for each level (math and language for example) are covered, but most of the time is spent on study that the student chooses. How this takes place is too involved to begin to cover here, but it is wonderful to see children embark on study that is way beyond what a teacher would require, just because they are excited about learning, and want to research and learn more and more.

*Each person's path is unique*

Each one of us is born with certain inborn talents, and our interests are aroused early in life, inspired by our parents, neighbors, and others. This kind of inspiration is the core of the work in Montessori. The teacher looks carefully for a student's learning style, learning needs, personality, and so forth, and offers work that will excite the student to want to do more, to learn more. It is exciting to see the variety of interests and passions, and the skills and abilities that result in this system of education. And it is exciting to realize that during a time when a student wants to focus on just one academic area, he will still be exposed, each day, to others being excited about other areas of study. This continually opens the door to more diverse and challenging exploration and learning.

*Montessori for family and community*

In the following chapters I will share details of the above—mixed-ages, everyday life skills, nature and local culture, enjoying academics, and an individual's unique path, and the natural impulse to be helpful —as they apply to the different ages and stages of life.

I hope that these ideas will enrich family and community life as more and more people see the potential of living and learning this way. I hope they will inspire creative ways to combine valuable traditions with mastery of the academic and scientific knowledge that can lead to a successful and enjoyable role in the unpredictable future, and to happiness.

*Times have changed, and science has made great progress, and so has our work; our principles have only been confirmed, and along with them our conviction that mankind can hope for a solution to its problems, among which the most urgent are those of peace and unity, only by turning its attention and energies to the discovery of the child and to the development of the great potentialities of the human personality in the course of its formation.*

—Montessori, *The Discovery of the Child*

# BIRTH TO THREE YEARS

*When does education begin?*

Even before birth a human being is learning by touching, seeing light and dark, and listening. The newborn has 100 billion neurons and is ready to start strengthening connections, that means he is ready to start learning. His education has begun.

He will learn about love and acceptance by how he is treated, how quickly and gently his needs are met.

He will learn to love and trust himself by how his attempts to develop—physically, mentally, and emotionally—are allowed and supported.

He will begin to learn about the world through experience in the world of the family and close community.

*Learning about our child through careful observation*

Observation is a skill used by parents and teachers at all ages and the more an adult learns the more easily an infant's needs can be met. Each cry is a message and adults can learn what is being expressed; is he cold or warm? Is there some discomfort of pressure or wetness? Is he unable to see something interesting? Is movement being impeded?

*Is Montessori expensive for this age?*
*A Mongolian example*

Sometimes one hears that it takes a lot of money to follow Montessori ideas in the home, but this is not the case. It is the continued learning of us adults—informing our support of his inborn drive to follow a unique path of development—that the child needs.

In 2018 I was in Mongolia to share Montessori ideas and to learn more about the child-raising traditions of this country. My hosts and I traveled far into the countryside to find a traditional family situation with young children. We found a family with two children living in a *ger*, or *yurt*, that was packed up and moved several times during the grazing season to follow the herd's need for fresh grass. The ger consisted of two beds, a table, a cooking/heating stove in the middle, an altar, and a few storage units for clothing, etc.

As the father was out with the animals we talked to the mother, a well-educated high school physics teacher who, along with her husband, choose to spend the summer months caring for family's herds of horses and yaks. She understood the value of a good education but, like many other people, thought that education begins around age six or seven years. Their plan was to move to the city when the children were old enough to attend school.

I wanted to learn about Mongolian practices, but soon we were into deep discussion about the first year of life, about the need for free-movement, and language, and how meeting these needs is not dependent on material objects, but on the knowledge, and observation skills, of the adult.

*Movement*

The four-month-old baby was tied to the wall of the tiny home so he wouldn't fall off onto the floor. He had been given a piece of dried yak cheese to chew on, an excellent tradition that strengthens the jaws and supports the even spacing of teeth later.

As we were speaking, I noticed the great effort the infant was making as he reached for and handled the cheese, and I suggested that we watch carefully to see what was going on. At times he held the cheese in his mouth and tasted it. Sometimes it fell to just out of his reach. At these times he used his whole body to reach and grasp it. His face was serious and determined; his wrist and fingers working hard; his whole body was rocking side to side to try to aid the reach.

I explained that this was just one example of extremely valuable developmental "work" and already an important educational experience. Neuroscientists tell us what is happening in the brain when the mind and the body work together to reach a goal: new pathways in the brain are being formed; skills are being improved; intelligence is improving. And very importantly, the young child is learning to trust himself, and to focus deeply. Because she was a scientist, this mother understood, and our discussion became very interesting.

*Traditions?*

We began to discuss traditions. There is great wisdom to be had by listening to elders in any community. However, sometimes there is a practice, a tradition, that was valuable in one situation, but not always.

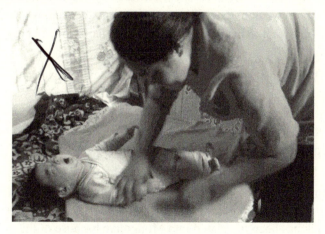

Swaddling, or wrapping a baby so securely that he is unable to move, is one of these traditions. I have spoken to friends who were swaddled when they were young during the Soviet Union era because during that time every adult was required to work every day, all day. There was no one available to watch over very young children, so there was very little free-movement, and more time sleeping adults could get their work done. Swaddling was the answer so the adults could get their work done.

As this mother showed us the tradition of swaddling it was very clear to all of us that this young boy had more important things to do, and he was very angry at being interrupted from his work!

I told her that even back in the USA today, some parents sometimes thinking swaddling is good for their babies, but more sleeping and less movement is not good for babies.

*Sleeping*

Montessori parents and teachers are aware that the human has inborn wisdom that tells one when to go to sleep, when to wake up, what to eat, how much, what kind of movement is valuable right now, and on and on.

It is a mistake to thinking of "putting a child to sleep,"—sometimes by swaddling and sometimes by nursing, or rocking, or even going for a ride in a car—when the best practice is to support the child in learning to put himself to sleep, and to wake up, following inner wisdom.

Here is a supportive quote from a Montessori teacher, mother, grandmother, head of school, from the book *The Joyful Child: Montessori, Global Wisdom for Birth to Three* (which has been translated into Mongolian because of this meeting):

*Please do not make our mistake of nursing Claire to sleep at night. In the uterus she had had lots of practice waking and going to sleep according to her mental and physical needs. Because I taught her to nurse herself to sleep, she became dependent on this and lost touch with her natural ability to go to sleep whenever she was tired.*

 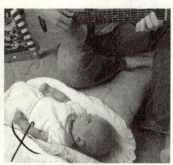

*Language and music*

I often try to imagine what it must be like, after months in the womb, to be able to see, hear, and touch the members of the family who one has already been listening to before birth. We observe that even a very young infant will stare closely at someone's face as they speak, appearing to connect the memory of this voice with the voice and face in the present moment.

Another support of language development can be seen at this young age, the attempt to imitate facial expressions and mouth movements of the other person. Such exercise of the mouth in imitation is a vital stage of the development of language. Because of all this important language exploration that is going on, we try—whenever a child is watching, studying, our face—to never look away until he does, until he is finished with his studying of our face or voice; for this is his most important education in the moment.

Singing a song to an infant that he has heard before birth can be very calming. This is the time to share the song, the music, even the musical instruments, of a family and the wider community.

*Motherese,* a way of speaking to a newborn with a high-pitched voice and simple sentences, is observed all over the world. It is an expression of adoration of a cute and helpless being, like the way we might speak to a new little kitten. It has its use for us adults when we spontaneously express our feelings when first meeting a new baby; but this has value only in the adult's first expression of welcome.

If we observe carefully, we will see that, even in these early months, an infant attempts to imitate our way of talking, and tries to communicate with us. Whenever we make eye-contact during the infant care activities of the day, such as changing a diaper or dressing, and try to imitate as closely as possible the attempts the child makes to communicate with us, we can truly engage in a conversation.

However, even from these first days of life, family and friends are modeling language, so we must try to remember to use the best, most precise, language—and speak in the same tone of voice we would use with each other.

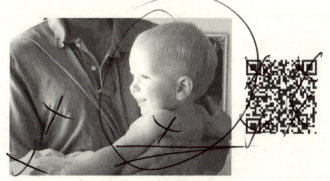

When our son, a musician, met his nephew for the first time he wanted to share his own joy of music. So, after looking through his sister's music cds he played short clips of music of many different kinds. Holding the child in his arms he moved with him to the rhythm of the music that was being played. Clearly the infant's brain was making connections between the sounds and the movements, each piece of music, and the accompanying movement, clearly enjoyed. This little boy is now in high school and very talented in music.

From the early days, an infant is learning the details of the language of the family and community, the objects and actions; the volume and tone of voice; the sentence structure; the vocabulary; and the musicality because each language has its own "song." Clearly preparation for speaking, writing, and reading, begins now.

One of the ways to support this stage of education is to tell the child what you are doing, and the exact names and adjectives of objects:

*This is a soft, blue jumpsuit that I am putting on you. Now I am snapping the buttons. Now I am going to sing a "dressing" song to you that my parents sang to me when I was a baby. I hope you enjoy it.*

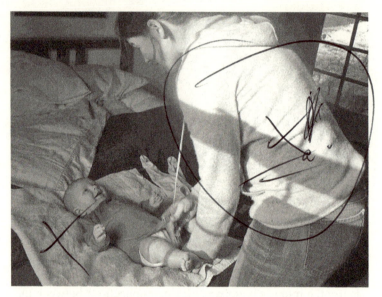

The more free-movement and exploration and interaction with people and in the environment, the more a child will want, and be able to, express in language.

*Movement and crying*

The director of my Montessori 0-3 training, Silvana Montanaro was an MD in the field of psychiatry, she told us that 50% of crying is eliminated by giving the infant the possibility of free movement.

*Safety*

As parents prepare for the child to join the family throughout the day, every bit of the room must be examined carefully to be sure that everything is safe to be touched by the infant—the floor, the lower walls, the furniture—because there are always unexpected leaps in physical ability when a child is allowed to move freely.

A father in Poland, who was using Montessori ideas at home with their new baby, sent me an amazing video of his son who was just learning to crawl. The infant slept on a mattress on the bedroom floor and even though the door to the rest of the apartment was left open the parents carried him to the living room to be with them when they heard that he was awake.

One day he decided to make the trip on his own. He crawled to the edge of the mattress and rocked back and forth, sometimes reaching down to touch the floor, as if he was judging the exact movement necessary to get to the floor. Occasionally he looked up at the dad and smiled but it was clear he wanted to do this on his own.

Finally, slowly, he touched the floor with both hands, pulled himself onto the floor, and crawled into the living room to join the family.

To encourage movement and inspire learning, we can place some touchable items on a low shelf in every room or arrange them in such a way that they can safely be handled by a child who is just learning to crawl and sit up on his own. This will give pleasure and encourage to use the hand in new ways. I once watched one of my grandchildren, who was exploring a shelf of bowls and other metal containers in our kitchen begin to match the size of a lid to different containers to see which would fit. This is an example of the development of the mathematical mind.

*Hands free!*

Sometime in the first year a child learns to move to a seated position on his own. There are many new activities that can be attempted now with hands free. And when there is a child-size table and chair available, the child can even begin to eat with a spoon and fork, pour himself a glass of water from a small pitcher, and serve himself food from a serving bowl.

How satisfying this must feel to be able to work on the skills he has observed in the family for months.

Montessori states over and over, in many ways, that there is a strong connection between the work of the hands and mental development. She points out that a child's intelligence, when helped by work with the hands, can reach a higher level and the character will be stronger.

*Pulling up*

The best situation for this practice is when a child can work on the new skill at any time, not dependent on someone else to pull him up.

Once I visited a family where there was a piano, clearly of interest to a child just learning to crawl. It was fascinating to watch the little girl pull herself up to the keys of the piano, play a note, carefully let herself down, and then repeat this cycle over and over.

It seemed as though the new movement challenge, and the music, were both calling her.

*First steps*

The path to mastery of the stages of language and movement in the first year are unique to every child. It seems that they listen to themselves and then decide what to work on next:

*Now I am going to spend my free-movement time to practice turning over, again and again and again. Oh, my mother is telling me the names of everything I can touch in the kitchen and that is just what I was interested in today. I am going to practice making the sounds I hear my family speak and sing all day. It seems that everyone around me is standing up and walking so today I am going to work on that.* And so on.

It is very important not to compare one child with another, but to learn to observe and take joy in what he is working on right now, and to accept him exactly as he is, and respect what he has chosen to work on in this moment. Then we can, without feelings of competition, enjoy what both our own child, and those of our friends, are working on at any one time.

The best situation is when a child is not rushed to learn to walk by being held— "helped"—by an adult holding him up to practice. If the adult patiently support a child's individual mastery of crawling, pulling up, and standing, then taking those first steps on his own is an experience of great joy.

Once the human being has learned to stand and walk the possibilities of development grow exponentially. This child will be able to imitate even more of what he sees going on in the world of the home and close community and, with a lot of forethought and planning on the part of the adults, will be able to participate and even contribute to the well-being of the group.

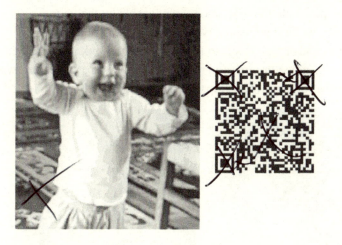

*First words*

Along with movement changes by the end of the first year, language takes a great leap. We might not understand what the child is saying to us, but we can make eye-contact, turn off our phones, listen, and engage more and more in conversation.

*At one year of age the child says his first intentional word . . . his babbling has a purpose, and this intention is a proof of conscious intelligence...He becomes ever more aware that language refers to his surroundings, and his wish to master it consciously becomes also greater . . . Subconsciously and unaided, he strains himself to learn, and this effort makes his success all the more astonishing.*

—Montessori, *The Absorbent Mind*

One of the discoveries Montessori made over one hundred years ago was that children would rather be doing the work that they see others carrying out, than play with toys. So, she began to have real tools created that were of good quality and a size that made the work more manageable by the young. Today we find items that were not available before: small tables and chairs, stools to reach the kitchen sink in the home, short-handled brooms and mops, even child-size wheelbarrows to haul soil and wood chips for the home garden.

Whenever one is carrying out a common activity at home, such as wrapping gifts, if a child wants to participate, one must learn to quickly analyze the steps involved and figure out which step will match the ability of the child who is watching and seems interested in joining us. One child will be able to smooth out the wrapping paper to be used, another is happy to hold down the gift as the adult ties the ribbon. As the child grows there will be more ways to participate in gift-wrapping, such as cutting the paper or ribbon, writing the gift tag, or tying the ribbon. This is a good example of the value of the adult learning to observe—discovering just where the child is at any given moment, because change is continual—and then figuring out what to offer.

### *The adult at home and in the Montessori infant community*

Before going any further I would like to point out that the trained Montessori teacher for this age is skilled at observations of this kind. She has nothing to distract her as she goes about her day combining knowledge of Montessori theory and what she sees is needed by each individual child at any one moment.

Parents or grandparents, on the other hand, have many roles to fill during a day. If there is time to begin to use all the ideas in the book all the better, but if not, just take time to think and perhaps try one tiny change a week. It is common knowledge that each person is doing the very best for his or her child with the knowledge, the time, and the energy, in the moment.

### *Exploring the culture*

While in Japan I observed a father or grandfather showing his very young son or grandson around a temple. There was a giant metal bell that was struck by pulling back a heavy rope attached to a very long and thick trunk of a tree. The adult showed the young boy how it worked and then the little one reached for the rope. The adult understood that he wanted to ring the bell, and so he handed it to the child and exerted just enough pull himself to ring the bell. The little boy left very satisfied with his success.

*Gardening and caring for animals*

There is plenty of work that could be shared both at home and in the Montessori class. Some examples are gardening and caring for animals. They can be done with the adult in the home but are usually arranged for the child to do at any time in the infant community. For example, after a lesson on picking cherry tomatoes there will be a garden basket available all day and any time during the day a child, who has learned to pick tomatoes carefully, can choose to do this work.

When feeding animals, the parent or teacher puts out the exact amount of food that the animal needs. In the infant community this usually means fish food to put in the aquarium, but in the home, it could also be for pets. Children quickly learn that when the day's food is out and ready anyone can feed the animal; and when the food is given to the animal, the work is done. The care and consideration of the animal is always the highest priority; an important lesson modeled for children.

*Flower arranging*

Flower arranging is a favorite activity in the home, the infant community and the Montessori primary class. The arrangement can be of whatever wild plants are blooming, flowers in the garden, or flowers brought into the environment by the adult, or even, when no flowers are available, a stem from a tree with leaves. The simple arrangements are often made of just one item that is placed in a small vase, given water, and then placed on the snack, lunch, or other table.

A friend once sent me a video of a young child doing the flower arranging work in an infant community. He was not yet a year and a half old and had been shown this work (given a lesson) by the teacher four months earlier.

A lesson in a Montessori class at all ages can be given 1:1 by the teacher, by another student, or even by carefully watching someone else doing the work. So, this child had clearly been watching and mastering some of the elements of the work—carrying items carefully, getting water in the bathroom, pouring water, placing objects carefully on a table, correcting mistakes such as doing the steps of a task out of order, and more. It was clear that he was thinking deeply about each step, making errors and correcting himself, being aware of the order and logic of the work, being flexible, remembering steps, deciding on and reaching goals, and throughout the whole work he was calm, patient, confident, working without frustration. This was a wonderful example of executive functions that is way beyond commonly held belief in the capabilities of a child under the age of two years.

Folding cloths in the infant community is one of many of the activities kept always ready and available on the shelf. But some folding is only carried out occasionally. An example is helping to put away the clean laundry. When a basket of freshly washed polishing cloths, hand towels, and aprons has been brought into the classroom it is placed on the floor near the area where these items are kept. Any child can then approach the work, remove one piece at a time from the laundry basket, place it on a table and fold it, sort it into piles, and then put everything away. Folding is a favorite activity and something that can be done at home.

*Meals*

Almost anything having to do with food is interesting at this age: planting and harvesting vegetables, cutting fruit, peeling eggs, arranging food on plates, setting the table, serving food, cleaning up after a snack or meal by washing and drying the table, sweeping the floor, mopping, and even washing the dishes.

Observing in a Montessori infant community I watched a very young child who was setting the table for lunch for the first time. He and the teacher each held a two-handle basket that was placed on the shelf. The teacher, and then the child, each placed only one plate in each of their baskets. Then, over and over, carried the plates one at a time to the lunch table, carefully putting them on the table above where each chair was placed. Then the plates were all set in place, they did the same with glasses, one at a time. And then spoons and forks. The teacher only collaborated until it was clear, with each new stage, that the child knew what to do, then she turned to something else, keeping her eye on him to be ready to show him the next step.

This kind of repetition, combining the work of the body (learning to walk while carrying something), the hands, and the brain, is a perfect example of real learning. It is also an early example of feeling useful and helping friends in the community.

*How to begin to offer real work in the home*

Figuring out how to include the child in the work of the family in the home is very different than in a classroom. The home environment is used by everyone at any age, and most work must usually be done efficiently and quickly, because there is so much to do in a modern home today. But there is usually a way.

We can start with one item, for example a floor broom with the long handle cut to a length so that a young child can use it—if a child-sized broom is not available. Prepare the broom and then decide on the most logical place to keep it. Fasten a short cord to the end, attached a hook to the wall, and show the child where the broom should be hung when it is not being used.

Just as in the classroom, in the beginning, the child will forget to hang the broom up when he is finished. In the classroom it might be another child who notices and puts the broom away, or the teacher, and gradually the child remembers that putting the work away is part of the work cycle and does it for himself. In the home a sibling or adult can also use this broom to sweep, and then put it away, modeling for the child who will eventually learn to do it.

Then perhaps think of the next task to prepare for the child's participation. The important thing is to observe the child's face as we carry out our daily work. If there is an interest, offer a way to participate. If it is possible for a child to choose a task at any time—for example setting a table which could be done at any time of the day—show the steps so the child can manage on his own. If not, joyfully work together.

*Why does the interest in a task wane?*

It is typical from this age through the primary class age of 6.5 years, that a child will master a task and then stop being interested. Even though we might expect that once a child, for example, learns to cut and arrange flowers to decorate the home or classroom, he will continue to do this. But this is not what happens.

The child at this age is working—from an interior guide—to master a task or skill. Then he moves on to the next challenge. We say that this child is not creating the environment, he is creating himself.

*Language – vocabulary*

All examples of work a child can carry out in the home and classroom, that were shared in this chapter, are enriched by learning the names of the objects and actions involved. With this vocabulary a child can explain what he wants to do, share his experiences, have more to talk about with his family. And each time a new word is learned, the connections in the brain are made more secure and important education has taken place.

Walking on the beach at low tide one day, with my two-year-old granddaughter, I pointed out the *bull kelp seaweed*, the *ochre sea star* (starfish), the *California mussels*, and the *green anemone* and invited her to touch these things. Then I gave her the name. Over and over, she touched and named, touched and named, and when we returned home told her parents about these creatures using the correct name. They were thrilled at her excitement about sharing her trip to the beach and astonished with her vocabulary. But these new words are no more difficult than the names of fruit and vegetables and clothing and cars, etc., and learning the vocabulary enabled her to tell her parents about the day.

*Books*

At this age vocabulary books are of great interest to the child, especially when they contain pictures of items he has seen in the home and community such as clothing, tools, farm animals, kitchen objects, etc. Look for pictures, if possible, with a white background behind the object being named, to avoid confusion. For example, if the bird is perched on a branch of a tree surrounded by leaves, exactly what is the parent pointing to when giving the name "robin?" Learning these words can increase the child's desire and ability to speak.

*Listening, the gift of our attention*

Even more valuable than modeling correct language and giving rich vocabulary, is the gift of our time and attention. It takes just a moment or two to halt the preparation of the meal, to bend down or sit so that our face is at a level as the child's face and make eye contact, when he starts to tell us something. Many families have a no-phone rule at meals and sometimes in front of young children. All Montessori schools that I know of have a no-phone rule during the school day. We adults are used to cell-phone interruption when we are with friends, but it is very difficult for a child at a young age to understand. The clear message is that for some reason, a small object has taken his parent away and he doesn't understand why.

*Music*

Music is so valuable that it should be modeled for the young before birth and then every day throughout life. Often, we adults most easily remember the songs we learned at a certain age, and sometimes they will even inspire us to dance. What an example for children in the home when we share music and dance that we love.

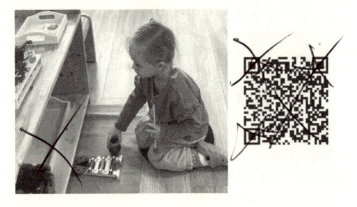

In a Montessori infant community, I watched a two-year-old spend a lot of time in the music area of the infant community. She laid out a small rug next to the music shelves, placed a container of musical instruments pictures on the rug, slowly look through them, and returned them to the shelf. Then, one at a time, she moved other items to the rug and explored them: playing each of the percussion instruments in a basket, and a small xylophone. After putting everything away, including the rug, she started singing a song and acting it out, "knees and shoulders, heads and toes."

This is a typical example of individual choice of work in Montessori classes. A child might have been introduced to songs in a small, spontaneously formed group activity with the adult, but singing goes on at any time of the day, as does all the other work.

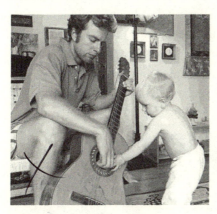

*Musical instruments*

There is so much recorded music available today that it is quite common for a young child to have no idea that it is the movement of the human body that creates music. Whenever possible try to show a child a real musical instrument. If a relative or friend plays an instrument, ask him or her to demonstrate it.

A child can be shown how to touch it carefully, sometimes even playing it. One child might be interested in learning the name of the instrument, and another the name and maybe even the names of the parts of the instrument; another child might be interested in the names of the notes played and the songs that are played. Follow the child.

*Avoiding praise*

When the child completes the work, we are very careful not to praise. We accept effort and work as normal for any member of the family or community. Most of all, rather than being in charge of what the child does, we try to protect the connection between the uniquely developing child and his own inner guide to choose work intelligently, concentrate, and create balance and happiness through his efforts.

Excessive praise can disrupt a child's concentration and even destroy his own intrinsic motivation for carrying out an activity, such as working hard or helping someone.

Working for the approval or praise of the parent or teacher can break the connection with the wise internal drive, making a child more focused on external validation. This can prevent learning and halt the development of independent thinking and responsible action. It is best, when we are sure it will not interrupt concentration, to just acknowledge effort, exactly as we might do with a friend who is pitching in to help, acknowledging effort without judgmental praise.

*Protecting concentration*

Over and over in Montessori theory and practice we hear about the value of concentration. Once a child has begun the work and is concentrating, we step back and protect the concentration, because deep concentration is a healing in many ways, at every stage and age of Montessori learning. As Montessori tells us, we must carefully work out an environment that would present the most favorable external conditions for this concentration.

*Concentration*

One of the most important results of Montessori practice, confirmed for over 100 years all over the world, is that the kindness, compassion, and a desire to help others, is an inborn characteristic of the human being. It appears following concentration. Not concentration on scrolling on a phone for example, but concentration that aligns with the stage of development of the individual, has been self-chosen, involves the mind and body working together toward an intelligent purpose, and that is protected from interruption until a personally set goal is attained.

Understanding the value of concentration can inspire us to look around the home or classroom, to carefully study the impulses of our child, and learn to figure out how to provide important work for a child and then get out of the way.

What better foundation for becoming a happy, confident, creative, and compassionate human being could there be?

In each of my talks over the years, and in most of my books I share the following quote:

*When the children had completed an absorbing bit of work, they appeared rested and deeply pleased . . . as if a road had opened up within their souls that led to all their latent powers, revealing the better part of themselves.*

*They . . . put themselves out to help others and seemed full of good will.*

*Thereafter, I set out to find experimental objects that would make this concentration possible, and carefully worked out an environment that would present the most favorable external conditions for this concentration.*

*And that is how my method began.*

—Montessori, *The Child in the Family (page)*

# AGE THREE TO SIX YEARS

*This is education, understood as a help to life; an education from birth, which feeds a peaceful revolution and unites all in a common aim, attracting them as to a single center. Mothers, fathers, politicians: all must combine in their respect and help for this delicate work of formation, which the little child carries on in the depth of a profound psychological mystery, under the tutelage of an inner guide. This is the bright new hope for mankind."*

—Montessori, The Absorbent Mind

In the 1990s after having taught children aged two through eighteen years, I attended a lecture given by Dr. Silvana Montanaro and Judi Orion, AMI Montessori teacher trainers. The subject was the child in the first three years of life. In the first slide, a two-year-old was reaching far down into a large aquarium. My immediate thought to myself was, "Oh, they are going to tell us what to do when a child attempts an activity that is beyond his ability." But that is not what happened.

They shared a series of pictures of the child removing most of the water of the aquarium—1 cup at a time—and pouring it into a bucket on the floor. Then he slowly and carefully wiped the green algae from the inside of the aquarium, took the bucket into the bathroom where he emptied it and filled it with fresh water, and refilled the aquarium, again one cup at a time. All of this was done without disturbing the fish swimming in a couple inches of water at the bottom of the tank. Finally, he wiped down the outside of the aquarium, with a child-sized wet mop cleaned spills from the floor, put everything away, and went on to other work.

This changed my life.

Some years later—after taking the Montessori birth to three course—I visited the first Montessori birth to three parent/teacher course that was being held in Japan. I observed a preschool that was gradually changing to a Montessori infant community during the year of the course.

I had never held a video camera before, but there was one available and I really wanted to share the amazing changes I was witnessing. After returning to the US, I filmed a Montessori infant community in Colorado. A friend helped me create a video combining footage from both Japan and Colorado to create a 1-hour introductory video of the 0-3 program. Today this video is available free on YouTube by searching "Montessori infant communities in Japan and the USA."

I am sharing information about the 0-3 program at the beginning of the Age Three to Six Year chapter of this book because, just as my life was changed after seeing the possibilities of work, problem solving, self-control, and deep concentration exhibited as that child cleaned out the aquarium, I saw the children in my primary and elementary classes as having far more potential than I had thought possible. I have shown this video in many countries and seen parents and teachers go through the same awakening as I did. I hope it is helpful to you.

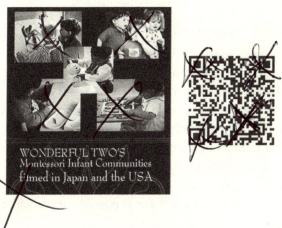

*Age three to six years introduction*

There are a few points to keep in mind as we consider how we can help our children develop fully during the last part of the crucial first six years of life. Just as in the first three years, this is the motor-sensorial time of life when a child learns through movement and physical senses. Also, this is the *absorbent mind* period of life because a child absorbs everything he encounters in the environment, even when it is an attitude or action that is not especially something we want him to absorb! If he attends a Montessori primary class, the environment will support the characteristics of the age. But if not in school, the more the parents and grandparents, the older siblings and close friends know about the physical, mental, and emotional needs at this time of life, the better will be the support. There are many exciting and enjoyable activities that the child, the family, and the close community can learn together that can fulfill these needs.

To begin, I will share some ways that a traditional preschool is different from a Montessori primary class preschool, and how much closer it is to the environment in the home.

### *The Montessori primary class*

Children enter the class, independently remove outer garments and sometimes change into slippers or "inside shoes," and greet the adults and other children just as they would if entering a home. They are free throughout the day to move about the room rather than being required to be silent and sit still in a chair or on the floor and listen to someone "teach" them or tell them what to do next; they can use the bathroom at any time without asking for permission; even choose to be inside or outside if this is possible in particular instances.

The education that takes place in a Montessori primary class for age 2.5-6.5, not only fulfills the needs of this stage of development but it is preparation for a happy and successful life in the future.

The following gives a brief overview of the lessons and activities in the Montessori class for this age. Some of these activities are already part of family life at home, and others could be, depending on the talents and interests of the family and community.

The areas are: (1) practical life, (2) sensorial, (3) culture, (4) language, (5) geometry and math.

### *Practical life*

If a child is hungry in the primary class, it is always possible for him to make and eat a snack; if he is tired or sleepy he can lie down and rest or sleep. One day I watched a child remove his slippers, curl up on the sofa near the classroom entrance, and close his eyes. Soon another child noticed and covered him with a blanket.

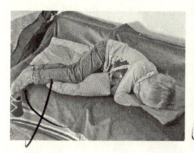 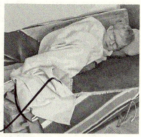

This is an example of participation in real family/community practical life work which includes: caring for oneself (learning to tie shoes, use a zipper, brush hair, etc.), caring for the environment (dusting, watering plants, cleaning windows, setting the dinner table, etc.); caring for each other (offering to help another who is in need, or to go to another child, or an adult, for help), and grace and courtesy, which means practicing graceful movement and good manners (how to carry water carefully without spilling, to offer food, greet a person just arriving, avoid interrupting someone who is speaking, or busy concentrating, etc.).

*Practical life while visiting grandparents*

By the time we had grandchildren visit us, my husband and I had much more time to prepare in order to meet their needs than when we were young parents. We had time to think about what possible changes to make in preparation for their visit.

Since we do not have a washing machine at home, when our visiting grandchildren wanted their clothes washed, they washed them themselves in the kitchen sink. Then I helped them tie a temporary clothesline between a chair and a deck post to hang them up to dry. On other days they washed furniture, dug potatoes, set the table, and joined in as much of the daily work as possible. One day, as I saw the eldest walking proudly through the living room I asked her, "Are you having a good day?" She paused a minute, and with a frown of deep thinking on her face, replied, "I shouldn't be, but I am!"

(What I imagined she was thinking, "Hmmm, children visiting their grandparents should be playing with toys, eating treats, and being entertained, but I am just working – and I LOVE IT!")

*Toys*

In the early weeks of the first casa dei bambini in Rome, there were typical Italian preschool activities much like in a traditional preschool, "gymnastics," playing with toys that had been donated, meals that had been prepared for them, marching, and free-play outside.

It was the children who asked to be involved in the real work: it was the children who, because of being allowed to collaborate in this work, lost interest in toys, and who no longer needed to be organized by an adult to participate in adult-scheduled group activities. Their day became very much like daily life in a home.

Toys fulfill a need in the busy modern home when parents are too busy to always include children in much of the family work: dolls, building blocks, beads to thread, games (especially cooperative games rather than competitive games). Some toys, such as knobbed puzzles, small beads for threading, and small colored pencils for drawing, contribute to a special skill of the fingers, called the pincer movement, that is preparation for writing with a pencil.

But beware of screens as toys because there is ongoing research that shows how young children are affected. In some countries it is recommended that children under six years of age have no, or little, exposure to screens. Our children are too precious to be experimented on with such technology.

*Sensorial activities*

The only activities in the first casa, and in Montessori classrooms, that are known as "didactic Montessori materials" are those that Montessori had used with children who were considered unable to learn. These materials are explored through specific activities that clarify sensorial concepts such as visual differences in colors, lengths, size; smells; sounds; and touch. They provide a child exacting challenges or goals when working with them. Through this work children reach a much higher level of intelligence.

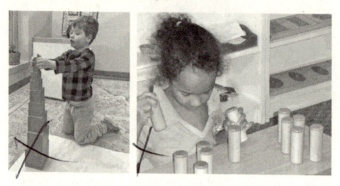

For example, the pink tower and sound boxes, or sound cylinders, are found in every Montessori primary class. When used correctly, following an exact lesson, these materials open a door to concepts that make one more aware of the world. Montessori teachers know exactly how to teach a child to use this material, enabling the child to abstract the concepts "large" and "small," (larger, smaller, largest, smallest), and, with the sound material "loud" and "soft" (louder, loudest, softer, softest). After the child has repeated and repeated the work, and seems to understand the concept, the exact language is given which adds to the rich vocabulary used in conversation and self-expression, and later writing and reading.

At home, when family members realize that such sensorial exploration is so important in the development of intelligence, they can look for experiences with items found in the home to help a child become aware of sensorial concepts. For example, cooking can be used to sharpen senses of tasting (sweet and sour, salt, etc.), seeing (color and shape), touching (hard, smooth, sharp, etc.), and smelling (the different odor of fruit, and food as it is being cooked).

The value of this kind of sensorial learning is profound and there are many reasons for providing it for children. The more aware a human becomes, at any age, of the details of the environment, the more the brain grows because of new connections, the more observant and curious he becomes, the more interestingly he speaks and understands the speech of others, and the more he can exist happily in the moment.

Field trips are generally not part of the Montessori primary class program. Instead, we speak of "bringing the world into the classroom." Going out into the community is a large part of the program after age six years. However, families often go to special places with their children, including museums. If planning a museum visit, look for those that have activities for children to do, not just look at. Sometimes there are wooden puzzles to put together, and drawers of items to touch such as shells, rocks, bones, books in a space for children to look through, and so forth. This will stir curiosity rather than create boredom.

In finding ways to help a child at home with sensorial exploration and education, I am not suggesting that, as in traditional education, the parent tells a child to sit down and listen and watch as the adult "teaches" him something. Instead, members of the family can begin to explore the home, to discover sensorial concepts connected with everyday life. Then learn to observe the child, to watch and discover interests, and then casually invite, offer, and include the child in new experiences, abstract concepts, and language.

The more aware a human becomes, at any age, of the details of the environment, the more the brain grows because of new connections, the more observant and curious he becomes, and the more he can exist happily in the moment. Not only awareness of the world, but language will be improved. Parents can engage a child in conversation about these sensorial experiences, intentionally using more and more interesting vocabulary.

*Culture*

In the culture area of the Montessori primary class there are experiences in physics, biology, history and geography, art and music, first examples from the child's own culture and country, and then examples from the wider world.

Many of the activities mentioned in this culture area are available in the book *The Red Corolla, Montessori Cosmic Education for Age 3-6+*.

*Culture – physics*

In the primary class, experiments are kept on a classroom shelf, and after having a lesson on how to carry out the experiment, children are free to work on them at any time. These concepts are explored: electricity, light and shadows, magnetism, the connection between air and water, a model of a Roman arch, magnification, sounds, objects that sink or float, pendulum, prism. With each activity there is specific practical life work, and—after the experience is repeated and learned—specific language.

When adults are studying to become Montessori teachers at this level, they spend many hours during the teacher training course practicing giving lessons to each other to be sure the steps are understood, and the materials work.

These adult students also practice, during a lesson, avoiding speaking and moving their hands at the same time. This is a very important skill to master because a child can focus on words or actions, but not both simultaneously. A child will not be able to focus and concentrate during a lesson if the adults speaks and moves at the same time and, as a result, will not be able to do the work well.

Parents can keep this in mind in the home when inviting the child to work.

I will give just one example from what we call "the world of physics:" assembling an electric circuit by carefully attaching the exposed ends of an insulated wire to a battery, a light switch, and a light bulb.

It is not so easy to get all the attachments perfect and this is the challenge, so there is often visible joy and excitement in the child's face the first time the switch makes the light bulb glow.

Changing the batteries in the flashlight at home is another opportunity to explore physics. Through trial and error, the child learns that the batteries must be placed in exactly the correct position for the light to turn on. Sometimes exploring a flashlight can turn into important physics exploration, requiring deep concentration, as a child takes a flashlight completely apart and assembles it himself.

Just a simple change in the environment such as making the on/off switch of a lamp available to a child is an experience of physics, the child learning the connection between the switch and the light being turned off and on.

Cooking as physics? Yes. One of my favorite memories of childhood is cooking with my grandmother, making noodles from scratch, but now I realize that it was also sensorial experience in physics, hard/soft, wet/dry, hot/cold.

After mixing the flour, eggs, milk, and salt, together we rolled out the "large noodle" on a floured surface. We had to keep checking the texture as we made it as large as possible. Then we placed a towel over the back of a kitchen chair and hung the large noodle over it to dry. It was my job to keep checking the dryness because if it was too moist the noodles would sick together when we cut them into strips. But if the large noodle was too dry the noodles would crumble as we cut them. This is physics! When it was just the right dryness (my grandmother continued to show me how to check both at the center and edge of the large noodle) we rolled up the large noodle and cut it into strips. Then we lifted the newly cut noodles a few times to be sure they are separated from each other, leaving them dry further. Some we cooked for dinner and the rest were stored in large glass jars for later use. Then there was the cooking, the boiling and simmering and tasting – all physics!

*Culture – biology*

Learning botany happens during gardening, growing vegetables, harvesting, cleaning, cooking, and serving the fresh food. These are activities that are carried out in many Montessori classes and can often be done together with the family at home.

In the classroom there are specific botany activities, experiments, demonstrated as 1:1 lessons, which then were at any time for a child to work with. They make clear such concepts as seed sprouting, phototropism (a plant growing toward light), and the needs of plant for light, warmth. These can be shown at home when there is a gardener ready to share her wisdom.

Here are examples of specific practical life activities in the area of botany that can also be part of the family work: raking leaves, cutting dead leaves or flowers from plants, watering plants, straightening up garden tools, cleaning, oiling, caring for garden tools, cutting and arranging flowers, changing water in the flower arrangements, dusting or washing the leaves of a plant, dusting or polishing the botany materials and the shelf where they are kept.

The language of this area is quite exciting and something any gardener in the family will enjoy, probably extending her own knowledge in the process. For example, a child learns the main parts of a plant (plant, root, stem, leaves, axis) and leaf (leaf, blade, margin, apex, base, stipule) and on and on. If the adult at home or in the community knows or is interested in this botanical information they can explore further with a child.

Nature walks and caring for and visiting other gardens becomes more and more interesting to a child after learning what to look for. There can be art projects connected with botany, for example cards made from pressed leaves. I have made cards with children from the pictures in seed catalogues.

Adult botany books with colored pictures are of interest to a child in this and in all these culture areas.

The zoology area of the classroom the work is like that of botany, including caring for the real animals, and learning related practical life and sensorial experiences, language, art, and books.

*Culture – history and geography*

Physical geography for this age means the geography of the land and water. As with all sensorial work, making the land and water forms in the sandbox, mud, or perhaps clay, is more important than just looking at pictures. Usually, island and lake are introduced first as they are complementary. This will make a child more interested in islands and lakes he hears others talk about.

Cultural geography at this age is based on exploring the physical needs of humans: food, transportation, housing, and clothing. First the child learns about these elements in his own family and culture, and then the wider world. Children never tire of hearing stories of what the older family members and members of the. community ate and what clothing they wore when they were young; how they traveled and what their homes were like. Children's books with good pictures of how these needs are met in other parts of the world are of great interest.

A globe combines the two: physical geography and cultural geography. Children can find examples of islands and lakes, capes and bays, isthmuses and straits, gulfs and peninsulas, and countries they have heard people talk about. Eventually these concepts and language provide very interesting subjects for a child to have conversations about and later write and read about.

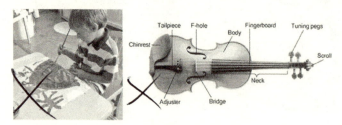

*Culture – art and music*

Every culture has its own art and music which is the best place to begin. Arts can include weaving, sewing, painting, making pottery, songs, dances—many examples of art and music of the family and community. Then examples from other cultures will be more interesting. Just as in all areas of culture, giving specific language—the names of art materials and colors when painting, names of musical instruments, even the names of the parts of a musical instrument – comes during or after the experience. This experience and vocabulary can awaken more interest in the child, and he can begin to include these concepts in conversations, and later writing and reading.

*Language – Listening, making conversation, and telling stories*

A child wants to know that what he has to say is interesting to someone, and that he will be listened to. This is the basis of wanting to speak. When a child feels that his ideas and words are interesting, he will be inspired to write. So, when a young child starts to tell us something, the most important thing we can do is, whenever possible, stop what we are doing, sit down with him, make eye-contact, and listen.

Songs, nursery rhymes, finger plays, stories from books are all important, but children really love hearing simple stories from the everyday life of their family and community. Here is an example from my own teaching years.

"One morning long ago, when my daughters were young, our horse, Bonnie, figured out all by herself how to get out of the paddock. She walked to the house, then made her around the back of the house where the kitchen was. We had just sat down to breakfast and were preparing to eat when suddenly, we heard a scratch at the window, looked up and, with great surprise, saw that Bonnie was looking in the window watching us eat!"

I have told this story hundreds of times, being asked for it by children in my primary Montessori class. The story was a little more detailed than what I have just shared but I learned early on that once the children learn the story, I had better not change one detail or they will correct me. You may have noticed the same request in reading a story to a child. Repetition is important at this age, and sometimes the first book a child reads will be one that has been read to him over and over and over.

This is so easy and important to do, both in the classroom and at home, enjoyable, and such a good model for a child when he sits down to compose and write his first story.

*Language – reading*

If we want children to read books, they must see others in the family and community reading books. Curling up in a cozy spot and being read to is one of the joys of childhood. In the Montessori class this happens between adult and child or a small group of children who gather spontaneously. And later it happens naturally between child and child, the older children reading to the younger.

*Language —writing*

If we want our children to be interested in learning to write with a pencil, they must see us writing with a pencil, perhaps a grocery list on paper like in the old days rather than on our phone. And if we want to inspire beautiful and clear writing, we can find a reason to show our children that we are still working on this, maybe when writing a thank you note for a gift.

One year when our grandchildren were visiting, we decided to write letters to my mother who lived so far away that we seldom saw her. Together we spread out the art materials on a table in the living room and began. Those who were not yet writing made drawings and decorated the pages that others had written. Over the years I have received a few hand-written thank-you notes from my children and grandchildren, and I still have each one and love looking at them. Such gifts are precious indeed.

*Preparation for writing*

One often hears the story of children magically discovering to write in that first Montessori school in Rome. This happens today in Montessori classrooms often around age four or four and a half. But that does not mean that one can enter the classroom at that age and begin writing! At least two years of preparation has come before this miracle.

Much of the practical work done in the classroom and home comprises this preparation—first they help a child master the movements of the whole body, then the arms, hands, wrist and fingers, all valuable for writing. Some activities in the home that help develop finer and finer control of hand and fingers specifically might be pouring, doing knobbed puzzles, stringing beads, sewing, drawing, coloring, painting, holding a nail to be hammered into a piece of wood, shelling peas, etc.

Learning a wealth of the vocabulary of the home and the cultural areas and being convinced that what he has to say is interesting, contributes to spontaneous interest in writing.

*Teaching the alphabet*

Society often promotes something that can cause confusion and difficulties in the process of learning to read and write. This is the teaching of capital letters and the names of letters first. In the Montessori class it is the lower-case letter that is introduced first (look at any book or newspaper or magazine and you will see how much more important it is to learn lower case letters) and the sounds (same thing – in reading we need to know the sound a letter makes, not the name of the letter). When the family understand this, the child will be better supported in preparing to write and read.

*Handwriting that a child is proud of*

Sandpaper letters are the materials used in the Montessori primary class for a child to learn the shapes and sounds of lower-case letters. These combine movement and touch and sound. The child is given a lesson on how to carefully and slowly feel the sandpaper shape of the letter while, at the same time, repeating the sound. This is an example of "firing together causes wiring together" or, learning and remembering. It teaches the brain to know that "ssss" is the sound of the letter "s," the connection is remembered because of the process.

*Rainbow letters*

One day a friend of mine who had taken over a Montessori primary class where the older children had bad handwriting asked me for help. Sandpaper letters are of interest to the very young child, but not to a 5-year-old. I suggested a method I have used in the same situation with good results.

I gave a child a container with 6-7 colored pencils, then very carefully traced the letter most troubling to that child while she watched carefully with great attention. I was very focused and a bit dramatic to draw her in, a skill used often in giving a lesson at this age.

After I had drawn the letter, about 4" tall on a single piece of paper, I invited her to do that same thing over and over, each time with a different colored pencil. This worked! She had created a rainbow in the shape of a letter.

It was not necessary to do this with all the letters because the child had learned, after tracing 8-10 letters, that she was perfectly capable of writing beautifully and thus began to write this way naturally.

Later I learned that my friend's students had also loved "rainbow letters" and she had helped them gather the finished pages into little books, complete with colored paper covers, and holes punched to allow ribbon to hold them together. Since then, I have heard that other teachers are also teaching "rainbow letters" to children in this situation. This is a perfect example of proof that the Montessori saying, "teach by teaching, not by correcting" is true. It is much more difficult to change a brain pattern than to carry out a task carefully and well in the beginning.

*Language – writing with original creativity*

While visiting a primary class in another country I watched a child carry a vase containing a flower to a table. Then she got out a piece of paper and a pencil. She looked at the flower and proceeded to draw. Below the image she drew horizontal lines and then proceeded to write something to do with the parts of the flower that she had drawn: corolla, pistil, stamens. This was in another language, so I could only decipher the labels of the parts which were in Latin, but she filled the page, put the drawing in a little drawer of her work, put everything away, and appeared deeply pleased.

I have seen many creative children's drawings, made with no suggestion by an adult. They are always much more interesting and varied than an adult might make. It brought home to me how important it is to encourage a child to draw, rather than supplying coloring books (at home) or prepared adult-drawn flowers, leaves, plants, etc., for a child to label, color in, and write about (in the classroom).

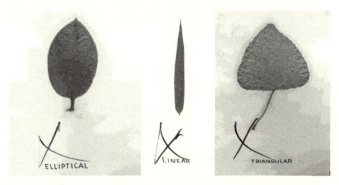

*Geometry*

In the Montessori primary class a child will explore, through special Montessori materials, plane geometry figures and solid geometric figures, and will learn to link them to the environment. For example, the leaf shapes in the classroom leaf cabinet are named according to their similarity to a geometric figure, including concepts such as linear, triangular, elliptical, orbiculate, ovate, and so on.

In the home, once we start looking, we see that geometry is all around us. The cereal box on the breakfast table? A square, a rectangular, and a rectangular prism. The doors, the windows, the dinner plates . . .

As with all lessons at this age, the experience comes before language. For example, we can point out similarities between an orange and a ball—if placed on an incline they will roll down the slope. After this sensorial comparison of the two, we can give the name "sphere." And look for other spheres: a globe, peas just taken from the pod.

My own father, a scientist, would have quickly pointed out the difference between a pea and an elongated spherical grain, an oblate spheroid, that is like a squashed sphere. But he quite often overwhelmed us with too much information whenever we showed an interest, which we learned not to do. That was an important lesson, teaching me the importance of not giving too much information even if we are excited about a subject, but instead to follow a child's interest, and allow discoveries at a child's pace.

*Math*

There are beautiful math materials in the Montessori primary class that introduce, and give hands-on practice, with counting, decimal system, and fractions. The most important consideration in the home—when a family want to help a child explore math concepts—is keeping in mind that at this age exploration is done through the senses, not mental abstractions unconnected with objects one can touch. Whenever counting together, arrange to touch the objects being counted, encouraging the child to touch each object as it is counted to make the connection with the quantity and the number spoken aloud. Fractions? We know that when an apple pie is served to six people at the dinner table, we are going to cut it into six equal pieces. We can casually point out that these are fractions called sixths.

In Bhutan, a country between India and China where children do not have toys, but spend their day interacting, and working along with family and community, children learn practical math very early. I saw a young child in an outside market shopping with her mother. Through my translator I found that they were discussing the quality of the produce, and the cost. The communication between them was clearly mutual respect for the other's ideas, and it was the child who counted out the coins and handed them to the farmer.

In a Montessori primary class one day, I watched the teacher write a short math story problem on a blackboard on the classroom wall first thing in the morning. By the end of the day someone had solved it and written the answer. This was a daily occurrence. The problems had to do with time, objects, amounts, fractions, addition, division, and any other math concept the children were learning about. There were only two or three sentences in this math problem and children in the class were sometimes mentioned. When the solution had been written no one commented, no child was praised. One usually didn't even know who had written the answer.

This was a perfect example of cooperation rather than competition in education, of approaching math as something completely unconnected with any stress or worry, but interesting, fun, and connected to everyday life.

*Concentration*

In Montessori practice at any age one of the main considerations is inspiring, and then protecting, episodes of deep concentration whenever they occur. Quite often we hear that it was a long, multi-step practical life activity that first brought a child to this experience. Once a child discovers how good it feels to deeply focus and concentrate deeply on interesting and challenging work, he will seek it out.

It is the Montessori teacher's main work to constantly observe each child, make written notes on work and levels of concentration, and figure out what 1:1 lesson to offer next. It is always the goal of the teacher to offer a lesson that is just the correct balance between too easy and too difficult—a lesson that is just right for that child at that moment.

When this work ceases, the children are gentle, calm and happy.

In Montessori's book *The Advanced Montessori Method* we have been given a tool that is used daily by many Montessori primary teachers. It is called a *work curve*. This is a graph that the teacher plots while observing a child's ability to concentrate. This observation helps the teacher offer work that will make it possible for a child who can only concentrate on easy work for short periods of time, to be able to carry out challenging work for long periods of time.

Montessori education has been described as a *restorative* education because, over time—through such periods of concentration on developmentally appropriate activities—a child becomes physically healthier, mentally calmer and more curious, emotionally confident, happier. He begins to enjoy silence, work, a love of order, profound spontaneous concentration, and he becomes more cooperative and kinder, looking for ways to help others.

This is not theory or fantasy, it has been observed millions of times, in children of all ages, all over the world. **In my mind this is the most important element of Montessori education.**

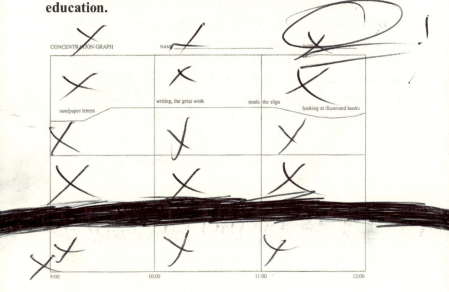

*Concentration in the classroom*

In my own Montessori classes I adapted Montessori's work curves calling them concentration graphs. Each day I tracked the work choices and the concentration depth of one child. It was thrilling to see that over the year(s), with no exceptions, the depth of concentration improved and so did all the other positive traits.

Here is a description of a typical day in my own primary class: arrival between 8:30-9:00. Free choice of work, inside or outside, no scheduled or required group lessons, until departure which was between 1:00-1:30. So the potential work period was five hours, but I tracked the concentration from 9:00-noon. Except for the beginning of the school years, there were no scheduled and required whole-group lessons or circle time, just spontaneous small groups organized usually by, or by request of, the children. Because by law we were not allowed to cook or clean anything to do with food (restaurant laws applied), children brought their lunch. So, at any time during these five hours children could have a snack (cutting fruit and putting peanut butter on crackers was allowed), set a table alone or with a friend, lay out food brought for lunch, eat, and then clean up. A child could lie down on a floor mat and rest or sleep at any time. This was indeed a real house of children, or casa dei bambini or house of children.

*Practices that can prevent deep concentration in the classroom*

Sometimes even us well-trained and experienced Montessori teachers, without the best intentions, speak or act in ways that prevent a child doing the kind of work that matches their stage of development and leads to deep concentration.

Here is an example:

The teacher says to a child who might be wandering, watching other, "You should find something to do." This will usually result in this child rushing to choose an easy task that does not challenge him or tach anything—to obey or please the teacher and look busy. This teaches a child that work in a Montessori class is often boring and unchallenging; and such choices will never lead to deep concentration.

In a work curve example in Montessori's book mentioned earlier, she write, in explaining what the child was doing at the end of the three-hour work period, "[the child] puts away work, contemplated his own work, and that of others."

Thinking about the work one has just completed, processing the experience, is very important and plotted as concentration. The brain is busy learning.

As another example, here is a lesson learned from a child.

Years ago, when I was teaching a primary class in my own school, I lectured on Montessori practice in the local college psychology, sociology, and nursing classes each semester. In the weeks following these lectures we usually had one or two students from these classes observing the classroom. The children had learned that these college students were there to learn, to take notes, and it was important work.

So, just as with any other important work, it should not be interrupted.

One day I watched a boy approach and sit on one of these college-student observation chairs and begin what was clearly an official observation. The other children recognized it as such and did not interrupt him. From then on, sitting on one of the observation chairs was valid work, bringing forth deep concentration, also inspiring learning through watching and deciding what work to do next.

Learning to not interrupt someone who is concentrating is a skill for the children. The adult always models it, not interrupting anyone who is working. We made a game of it, practicing different ways of watching work we were interested in while not interrupting. Sometimes a child would move a chair two or three feet away from a child, sitting quietly, and watching. This was valid work and a lesson. Sometimes a child would see how close he could get to another child's work without being a distraction. The working child would continue with the assurance that he would not be interrupted.

In my home? Well, I am still working on this. I still sometimes call out to my husband without considering what he may be concentrating on. At least he has learned that, if he was busy reading or working on something when I call his name, he can continue his work and answer at his convenience. When my grandchildren are visiting, however, I can be the perfect grandmother and pay close attention to what they are doing before I call out their names.

Being a retired or semi-retired grandmother or fulltime Montessori teacher is so much easier in many ways than being a parent!

*Inviting rather than ordering/directing a child to work*

Here is another example of teacher's words that can prevent deep concentration. Never would a teacher say, "Come with me . . . I want to show you something." In every instance we invite a child to an activity in the classroom rather than telling the child what to do. The teacher finds many ways to invite, to offer a lesson to a child, rather than ordering a child to do something. An example is, "Would you like . . .?" or "I have something to show you . . ." or "I have been thinking of something you might like . . ." and so on. This becomes second nature. The Montessori teacher would avoid saying, "Put that there." Instead, "This belongs here." We teachers are always learning ways to invite rather than direct.

Such careful changes in our language support a child's intelligence, independence, and skill in making the right decisions.

There are some lessons and games where there is an unspoken agreement to use directives (the verb game for example where a child reads the card, "jump" and his fellow student follows his direction) or the rarely carried out, very special silence game where the teacher whispers, "Come to me." To each child.

Otherwise, it is a vital element in Montessori practice that aids a child developing confidence to choose, to make his own decisions. Speaking this way shows respect in the process and in the child; it is interpreted as our having trust in him and will lead to better choices and deeper concentration.

Here is an example from a home. One year I was staying with a mother who lived alone in an apartment with her four-year-old son. He had climbed up on the kitchen counter, and then to the top of the refrigerator to get to the cookies he knew were there. He almost fell and could have hurt himself. She was frantic and asked for my help.

Throughout the next day I wrote down each time she told his son to do something, each directive or order. At the end of the day there were more than 80 examples. We looked at them together and discussed examples of better wording, invitations and choices rather than directives. For example, "Wash your hands and come to dinner." could be, "Dinner is ready; are your hands clean?"

Otherwise, such seemingly small orders as "pick up your socks" are interpreted by a child as equal in importance to, "Don't ride your bicycle in the street." Or "Don't climb up on top of the refrigerator."

In the class and at home, learning to replace directives with invitations takes some effort, but it is very important.

*When a child asks for a lesson that he is not ready for*

Another sentence we don't hear in the Montessori class is, "You are not ready for that work."

For example, a child takes the teacher by the hand and leads her to the large, beautiful bead cabinet that is very attractive to a three-year-old, but a year or more away in being appropriate work for this child. If we say, "You are not ready .

. .," as an adult we know that there will come a time in the future when this child will be ready. But what this young child, with no understanding of the passage of time, hears is, "You will NEVER be ready for this work."

What do we do? Sometimes I have shown a child in this situation how to dust the bead cabinet (and other material she is not yet ready for) and often this is satisfying. But if the child has already begun the math work, working with the number rods for example, we can say, verbally matching the obvious excitement of the child who is attracted to these materials, "YES! You will be able to do this work. First, you can get started on this other work to get ready for the bead cabinet work (pointing to math materials that must be mastered first). Shall we begin now?" And then, give this child the lesson that will eventually bring her to the large bead cabinet.

In the home it is quite common for a child to compare himself with a slightly older sibling and see that the sibling can do a lot that he cannot. He thinks it will always be the case. When the family are aware of this, just as the teacher in the classroom, it can be explained by offering something similar with the assurance that this alternate work comes first and will prepare the child who will someday do everything the older sibling is doing.

### *Silence or noise, and still concentration*

Most of the time when entering a primary or elementary class visitors are struck with the silence. I have even heard it said that "These children must be hypnotized." This is not an imposed silence. The teacher does not go around the class and tell children to be quiet. Instead, she observes the noisy child to see what is causing the lack of quiet that one expects during deep concentration. If the noise is the result of the excitement of a discovery, or laughter because of a humorous situation, or natural conversation during an activity a few children decide to do together, this is not a problem.

But if it is the sound of chaos caused by boredom, perhaps caused by a bad match between child and a task, or an unwelcome interruption of someone whose work might look more interesting, she makes a note and as soon as possible decides what she needs to offer next, work that will provide the perfect challenge.

It is lovely to see a child who can concentrate deeply with the sounds of normal activities going on around her—because she knows that everything is fine, everyone is safe.

*Concentration at home*

In a Montessori class it is the teacher's profession, her work, to stay focused all day on meeting the needs of children; this cannot be expected of parents and other family members who have so many responsibilities in the home.

But I hope that all the examples of activities in this chapter will inspire family members to discover ways to include the child in the daily life of the family. It is a joy to discover how capable our children are and how kind and helpful children naturally are when their needs are met; to learn that this is the normal behavior of the human being.

# MY PRIMARY AND ELEMENTARY MONTESSORI CONSULTANT AND MENTORS

*Margot Waltuch—my AMI consultant*

Margot Waltuch, in the 1970's, was the official AMI consultant for my primary class in Michigan, and later for my elementary, age 6-12, class in California.

Margot was first Froebel trained. The German Friedrich Froebel was a student of Pestalozzi who influenced Montessori's ideas. He created the first kindergarten, a place where children could develop at their own pace. Then Margot earned an AMI diploma in Rome in 1930. She had a French degree from the Sorbonne in Paris, taught children in Montessori classes in France, and became Montessori's official translator and fellow researcher for teaching materials in Holland. She earned a master's degree at Columbia University Teachers College and lectured there.

She was the AMI consultant for schools in the USA, Europe, Japan, Canada, and Mexico. She was a delight to spend time with and I was very fortunate to have her as my consultant.

### Margot's consultation for my primary class

The children arrived between 8:30 and 9:00. Lunch would be at noon. Margot and I watched the children through a 2-way mirror between the coatroom and the main classroom as they entered the main room and began their work. There were thirty children between the ages of 2.5 and 6.5; the assistant was nowhere in sight. After a little time, Margot turned to me and said, "They don't seem to need you." I was surprised at this comment because my class was just like the classes I had observed and in which I had student-taught during my training in London; I expected my students not to need me.

Around 11:30 I gathered the children for "circle time." This was something I dreaded a bit because I had discovered that there is no way a person can successfully teach or entertain a 2.5-year-old child and a 6.5-year-old child at the same time, with the same information or activity. After a few moments, Margot turned to me with a frown on her face and said, "Did you learn this in your London training?"

My reply, "No, but I thought I was supposed to do it. Do you mean I don't have to?"

Margot, "No! And I don't know where this American 'mother and chick' practice came from, but it has nothing at all to do with Montessori!" That was such a relief.

During our meeting at the end of her consultation, the only negative comment she shared was that my older students could be working at a higher level than they were at present. She assured me that this would happen naturally since morning group was now eliminated, because the children would have more independent work time and would be able to tackle and complete more advanced work.

She was very interested when I explained where my "mother and chick" practice had come from.

It had started in 1971 in San Francisco, the year following my training in London. In this new class there were twenty-five children, ages 3-6, all new to Montessori, five full days a week. A few weeks into the year, the head teacher at the school who also oversaw other teachers because of her own training (3-6 in London and 6-12 in Bergamo, Italy) and years of teaching experience, observed my class.

At the end of the morning, when the children were having lunch, she told me that everything was good, but I should gather the children at the end of each morning for a whole group circle time. This was a new idea for me, but I was sure that she knew more than I so I obeyed.

As a result of this guidance, I gathered children for circle time every morning in this school, and later in my own, until Margot brought me back to authentic Montessori practice.

*What changed after Margot's visit?*

Because the parents of my school were already thrilled at what was happening to their children, and because they trusted me, they allowed me to experiment with the schedule, and the ages of the children in the class.

As a result of the lengthened work-period with no scheduled, teacher-led, group lessons (from three hours to five hours), the more the children accomplished in all areas and the more deeply they concentrated. The wider the age span (from the day after a child's second birthday until almost seven years of age) the more the social atmosphere changed. It felt like a new baby being welcomed into a loving and supportive family. These changes provided more physical, mental, emotional, and spiritual support for everyone.

Over the years since then, I have shared her wisdom and my own experience in many countries, as a speaker and school consultant—this information is always met with relief when teachers realize they can give up the existing daily scheduled circle time. (In the Age Three to Six Years chapter of this book there is more information about the class that Margot observed.)

*Margot's consultation for my elementary class*

Years later, in my 6-12 class in California, Margot was brought in as the AMI consultant for the whole school. She was pleased to see my class devoid of scheduled, adult-led group lessons of any kind. She visited with the children and enjoyed the unique creations/projects they were designing, their excitement about their work, and the kindness with which they greeted her, and treated each other.

*Some of my other Montessori mentors*

Karin Salzmann was the founding executive director of AMIUSA and brought Mario Montessori to the USA to inspire us. She was responsible for bringing Silvana Montanaro, MD to the USA in 1979 for a workshop that led to Montessori 0-3, or Assistants to Infancy, teacher/parent training in our country. Karin moved to our town in 1999, and we worked together in many countries as speakers and oral examiners for 0-3 courses. She edited my first two books and inspired my continued writing.

There are many people who have mentored me over the years; here are just a few Montessorians that I cannot leave out of such a list: Annette Haines, Joke Verheul, Lynne Lawrence, and Judi Orion. They have always been there for me whenever I had a question when writing, preparing a lecture, or consulting. The question might be about the source of a quote by Montessori, historical accuracy, or authentic Montessori practice in the home or at school.

Professor Adele Diamond, who has referred to herself as "a Montessori groupie" is a pioneer in developmental cognitive neuroscience. I have been so lucky to spend time with her in the Netherlands, Sikkim, Thailand, and Canada.

She has taught us even more about the value of Montessori: the clean, ordered, and uncluttered environment reduces stress; mixed age groups and peer learning/teaching that is cooperative rather than competitive prevents the stress of loneliness; studying music and dance, the arts, and sports all emphasize developing skills over content, and are perfect examples of multi-step challenges that improve executive functions.

*Montessori teacher trainers and examiners*

*0-3 course*: The directors of the training course I took in Denver, Colorado were Silvana Montanaro and Judi Orion. At the end of the chapter Age Three to Six Years I share how instrumental both women were in my work.

*3-6 course*: for my 3-6 course in London—which had been created by Mario Montessori—Hilla Patell and Muriel Dwyer were the directors of training. Later my husband and I worked with Muriel and NAMTA (North American Montessori Teachers Association) to bring her system of reading and writing to the USA. My last physical contact with Hilla was during the Montessori congress in Prague where we spent three days together, and I have fond memories of our long conversations (Hilla calling from Oxford) as I prepared to deliver the London course culture lectures at the first 3-6 course in Morocco.

*6-12 course*: the 6-12 director of training was Margaret Stephenson from the UK. The oral examiners were Mario Montessori and Albert Max (Abs) Joosten who was one of Maria Montessori's earliest students and a key trainer, particularly in India and Sri Lanka.

Mario Montessori was my oral examiner for the math area. Yes, I was nervous!

In a Montessori oral exam, a person draws a slip of paper

from a basket containing several—each with the name of one of the lessons in that area to be examined. This ensures that no one knows ahead of time what will be the subject of her oral examination. For the math area I drew the lesson called *the checkerboard*. This is a long lesson that takes up three pages in my math album; it has at least fifteen exercises and passages; the work can be spread over days or weeks, following the child's interest and mastery of the work; it provides experience with hierarchies in the decimal system beyond the thousands, relates multiplication to geometry, and prepares a student for the square root work.

Mario was gentle, brilliant, patient, and kind, and my time with him helped me understand, and appreciate more deeply, the reasons why lessons are given always to one child at a time. Today neuroscientists can explain executive function of the brain, something that Montessori seemed to intuit so long ago. Now we understand Montessori practice scientifically and in a new light.

Mario did not use the same language, but he made it clear that since math calculation can easily be done by an electronic device, solving a math problem or mastering academics of any kind is not the most important reason for the work in the Montessori elementary class.

When a math problem with many steps such as the one we were discussing is carried out over a long period of time by just one child, it exercises many parts of the brain and leads to deeper and deeper levels of concentration and greater intelligence and happiness. The aquarium-cleaning example of the very young child in the introduction to this book is an example; the complexity of the challenges, and the satisfaction one feels upon their completion, continues to grow over the years.

When I think back over my elementary students' work in all areas, I am struck by the support for the brain that is inherent in multi-step challenges, and I understand the value of so much independent work in an environment that supports deep, uninterrupted concentration. All the following executive functions are improved: self-regulation, planning, focus, remembering instructions, managing multiple tasks, skills like working memory, cognitive flexibility, and inhibition control. All of this is so much more valuable than following a prescribed academic curriculum.

When parents realize this, they also can appreciate the value of children working along with the family in long and demanding tasks and projects.

*My own work with parents and teachers around the world*

So, you see, the words in this book are not just my own private information. They come from the experience and deep wisdom of many people; wisdom that can help us parents, grandparents, and teachers continue to develop ourselves as curious, intelligent, and wise human beings who are willing to be wrong, to study, and to try over and over to be the best that we can be.

Then we are prepared to observe and learn from watching our children and students and fully support them as they learn to follow their own valuable and unique paths, becoming life-long learners, creative problem-solvers, compassionate, happy, and kind individuals.

> *The real preparation for education is the study of oneself. The training of the teacher [and parent] who is to help life is something far more than the learning of ideas. It includes the training of character; it is a preparation of the spirit.*
>
> —Montessori, *The Absorbent Mind*

# AGE SIX TO TWELVE YEARS

I have written about this age in several other books and am including a few quotes in this chapter. Understanding the characteristics of this age, and how the daily practical work and academics are approached in a Montessori 6-12 class, will give parents, grandparents and others in the community ideas on how to enjoy, and explore life with, children at this age.

*From independent learning to the factory model and back*

Montessori is not the only educational system focusing on independent learning, peer teaching, mixed ages, and offering more than academics. Many families, communities, and educators are experimenting today and learning from the past.

From Professor Angeline Lillard's book *Montessori, the Science Behind the Genius* (the chapter "An Answer to the Crises in Education"):

*Prior to 1850, the one-room schoolhouse was the dominant form of schooling in America. In such environments, education could be individualized, a wide age-span of children occupied a single classroom, and teachers had significant independence in carrying out their didactic duties, responding only to a local board of directors. From the mid-19th century on a change gradually took place as mass public schooling swept across the United States (and Europe). This coincided with the age of efficiency, in which a great deal of public discourse was focused on how to streamline business operations for maximum efficiency. Simultaneously, waves of immigrants were arriving on US shores, intensifying the pressure for mass schooling.*

*Because of this temporal synchrony, modern schools were consciously modeled on factories, with their priority of efficient operations.*

*The whole class teaching is convenient for teachers and sensible if one has a particular model of children as learners, but it also has high costs for children. Children of the same age are often at different levels within a topic. They can have different interests, which makes them benefit from somewhat different teaching. They can learn at different speeds and can be helped tremendously by interacting with other children who are older and younger than themselves. Whole class teaching fits the factory model well, but not the child.*

My husband's mother was a teacher in a one-room school in Minnesota. Our family members have visited a preserved one-room schoolhouse in that state, and I have visited one here in California. One of the elements that we all found most striking was the textbooks. The level of a well-rounded education reached was surprisingly high, and the family were unable to answer all the questions in typical academic tests! Also, there was an emphasis on honesty, goodness, and being a helpful person.

We would find the same thing if we took a test of the material covered by the end of an age 6-12 Montessori education, I am sure. And, like the results of a Montessori elementary education, because of the way learning took place (1:1 lessons, peer teaching, no 50-minute classes, cooperation rather than competition, time to do the work), much more of the academic content was successfully learned and remembered.

Recently I read an article in the Humboldt Historian (Spring 2025) rich with memories from farm life in the 1920s and 1930s, by Gerould Smith.

Here are some facts and quotes I have gathered from these sources to give you some insight into one-room school education:

—The schoolhouse interior was often more like a living room, only sometimes containing desks.

—The teacher arrived early to start the wood fire; she often boarded with the family of one of the students.

—Ages in one class ranged from 6 years through 16. The number of students varied greatly each year.

—Seldom were there more than one or two students at the same grade at any one time.

—Students oversaw gathering and maintaining wood for the fire, cleaning up after themselves, cleaning the room, the blackboard, etc.

—The teacher would move from student to student throughout the day giving 1:1 lessons.

—The younger students were daily exposed to what the older students were learning, inspiring curiosity and passive learning. The older students often helped and taught the younger.

— (Gerould Smith) *At recess and at noon time, we set out lines for trout in the Eel River. Usually, we baited them with bread. Often, we went home with trout or suckers. I started grammar school as a second grader because Mother had taught me to read, spell, and write. There were about fifteen students from eight to sixteen years of age. The county school superintendent from Eureka visited all small and one room schools in the county twice a year. He would check records with the teacher, and the students would read and do math on the blackboard while he observed. At the end of the visit, he would write the name of a student that he thought had performed well in large, sweeping, shaded script on the blackboard. It was left there for a week or two. Everyone agreed it was a special honor.* (Gerould Smith went on to earn three degrees at Stanford University and became a research chemist.)

*The family and community as models*

In the first six years of life the family and community are the most important teachers. But that should not end at age seven. The needs of the child and young adult, between birth and age eighteen change significantly over the years, and the more the family and community understand these changes, the better models they will be, and the stronger will be the bonds and support among all members of the group throughout life. As adults we are always the model for our children and students, even if it seems that they are not watching us.

As a Montessori teacher I often do things I love in the classroom, such as playing the piano or guitar, because I knew my love of such activities was a good model for the children. When teaching in a primary class I looked forward to hemming dusting cloths and polishing cloths during quiet moments in the classroom, for my own pleasure, and to show the children that sewing is real and important work, not just a classroom activity.

*Concentration and Silence*

There is so much interesting knowledge covered during Montessori 6-12 training, that sometimes it is difficult to put that focus aside and look for instances of deep concentration and the resulting silence when children are working. Love of silence is one of the characteristics of a child becoming truly balanced and happy that Montessori often mentioned; she observed even in her lifetime that *silence is missing from our lives*.

Spending time in nature outside the classroom is helpful in this regard. For myself, my happiest memories from childhood at this age were not the times spent with other people at parties or in school. My happiest memories were at my grandparents' farm climbing alone into the barn loft to play with kittens; cooling off in the icehouse where the milk was kept cold; walking along the riverbank singing; and climbing as high into the branches of a tree as possible. Think of this when you notice one of your children or students seeking out a private, quiet place.

When I am speaking, I often show a short video of a primary class where the adults are mostly out of sight and the children are going about the day, choosing work, concentrating, and even watching another person carefully before speaking because they have learned the importance of not interrupting. In this video the children have been given many 1:1 lessons and have many activities from which to choose.

However, in Bhutan I once filmed the very first day of the first classroom in the country run by a Montessori trained teacher. There were very few "Montessori" materials, mostly simple bead stringing, sorting objects and puzzles and practical life. The children were welcomed into the classroom one at a time, invited to choose a floor mat or table mat, and then to select one of the activities and take it to the place they had chosen to work. The teacher gave a brief 1:1 lesson on how to use this material and explained that when they were finished, they could take it back to the shelf and choose something else.

The children responded beautifully, walking carefully and handling the objects with respect. Such results are the same all over the world—because Montessori practice is natural to the child.

The parents crowded around the one window through which one could observe the class from outside the school in amazement. They had never ever thought that their children would be able to walk so carefully, choose work, be so calm, and concentrate.

*Keeping this concentration in the elementary class*

Now, just as during the first six years, deep concentration is valued above and beyond the content of an academic curriculum. At any age, when a person embarks upon a project—in the home or at work—and can focus on it without being interrupted, and feels satisfied at its completion, the result is usually calm and happy feelings.

In my experience as a school consultant, I have sometimes found that an elementary teacher who has already experienced such concentration and silence as a primary teacher, has an easier job of creating the same situation, in the elementary class.

> *My teacher trainer, Miss Stephenson, was visiting an elementary class. It was one of those classes where children, almost all of the children, are talking all of the time. After some time, she couldn't take it any longer and she stood up from the chair where she had been observing in the middle of the room and called out, "Be quiet."*
>
> —Stephenson, *Montessori and Mindfulness* (chapter "Work as Mindfulness")

*Age 6-12 characteristic—behavior changes*

At the beginning of the age 6-12 stage of development, there is an exploration of society including all kinds of behavior, good and bad.

I once had a child in my primary class who entered the local public school at age 6.5 and, according to the parents, was turning into a rude and misbehaving child. I was glad to have the chance to explain to them that it is normal at this age to try out the behavior seen around one. A child might hear another child swear. He comes home and swears at dinner. Then turns to his parents with a questioning look on his face as he waits to learn from them.

Parents and teachers must set limits and teach good behavior, but when we understand what is happening, rather than teaching by punishing or by ordering "time out", we can sit down with our child and talk about what he saw and might be trying out at home, and everyone can share their opinions on what constitutes thoughtful and polite behavior.

*Age 6-12 characteristic—an interest in fairness and justice – in school and in the home*

Tattling is another common behavior now, both at home and in school. The child comes to the adult and tattles on someone. Most of the time he is asking for help, for advice, for information about what is right or wrong; he wants to know the opinion of the adult he is tattling to. Understanding what is behind this behavior guides the adult to a solution that ends in knowledge, self-respect, and respect for others.

From my book, *Montessori Cosmic Education, The Child's Discovery of a Global Vision and a Cosmic Task* (chapter "Making the World a Better Place, Six to Twelve+ Years"):

*At this age there is a natural interest in fairness and justice in the classroom and in the world. The level at which children can care for each other and for plants and animals and can go out into the world is much higher. They can clean the beaches and riverbeds, feed the homeless, cook their own meals, and clean the school. When there is a temptation to focus on the academic curriculum at this stage these things must be kept alive.*

*It is easy for us parents to fall into the habit of doing all the real work in the home, "You do your homework, don't worry, I'll do the dishes, I'll clean up the kitchen or the bathroom, mind your little sister, do the vacuuming, laundry, etc." and then to get upset because the children don't do any work around the house!*

I have never liked the word "chores" in referring to the daily life in the home as it has such a negative connotation. I have watched families struggle with rewards and punishment, and trying to make the child guilty, and then just giving up and doing the work themselves.

One year I came up with a fun plan that has helped many families study the balance of work in the home as a group, and then divide the work, always listening carefully to the input of the child. You can read the details of this project in the "Fifth Grade" chapter of the book *Montessori Homeschooling*. Here is how it came about:

One year we had a visitor in our home who never offered to help in any way and was not really liked by others as a result. It was clear that she had been raised that way. I didn't want to hurt her feelings, but I wanted to figure out a way for her to discover how out of balance this was. I decided to create a project that would make it clear just who was doing which work. I designed a form that tracked the amount of time a person spends in activities such as: helping family or community, working at a job, studying, being at school, reading, practicing a skill, leisure activities, "hanging out", TV (now I would list screen time), sleeping, bathing, eating, dressing. Everything is color coded—a very mathematical, interesting, and fun exercise. After each family member fills out their own form they compare, always with many discoveries and surprises, and always with a newfound awareness of just how much work goes into running a home, valuable information for now and for the future.

*Age 6-12 characteristic—independence in problem solving*

This is an example from a colleague:

*There were papers strewn all over the classroom for the last couple of days. I wondered why the children had not been filing their work papers. However, I made a deliberate effort to not address the problem but waited for the children to bring it up themselves. It finally happened at the end of the week during the class meeting. Two of the children stood up and questioned the whole group, "Why are there so many unfiled papers lying around?" What followed was an outpouring of opinions, complaints and confessions, and within a few minutes of the whole class discussion, they came up with the root cause of the problem.*

*The punching machine that was supposed to sit on a tray in a particular spot kept moving around!*

*Elementary children are problem solvers, they are quite capable of finding solutions to everyday situations – a broken clothesline, a messy shelf, conflicts between friends. They are also capable of looking at the big picture, seeing problems in the community and coming up with solutions for them. They are a perfect blend of intelligence and creative thinking and at this age, they are enthusiastic and hard-working and have a desire to contribute. The thoughtful and logical ideas that they come up with during discussions, whether it is the day to day working of the school environment or matters as profound as the worldwide waste generation, have always amazed me.*

*So true are Dr. Montessori's words: "THE CHILD IS BOTH A HOPE AND A PROMISE FOR MANKIND." (from her book Education and Peace)*

I gave two good examples of the students solving problems in the book *Please Help Me Do It Myself, Observation and Recordkeeping for the Montessori Primary and Elementary Class* (last chapter of the "Elementary, Age 6-12" section)

It was my first year of teaching elementary and ours was a class of children ages 6-15, many of the students completely new to Montessori. I will share two stories about what I learned from the students.

Early in the year the new-to-Montessori students called a meeting and discussed the fact that they were used to more teacher-assessment and rewards for good work, and they were having trouble completing the week's work without approval or reward (the work was based on an individual meeting I had with each student once a week to together come up with a study plan). I put the problem into their hands, and they ended up being able to complete their own work each week with no rewards, and helped others complete theirs.

Later in the year I was sick for three days. I never had an assistant at this level so—with permission from me and from the head of the school—since there were no scheduled activities for the week and the students each had their own plan of study and work, they were completely in charge of themselves for those three days. At the end of this time, I had learned a lot about the potential for independence and responsibility at this age and so had they.

> *Blessed are the teachers who have brought their class to the stage where they can say, "Whether I am present or not, the class carries on. The group has achieved independence.*
>
> —Montessori, *Education for a New World*

*Age 6-12 characteristic—forming groups, the children's responsibility*

Working together is one of the characteristics of the 6-12 stage that has been observed in Montessori classes worldwide. But it is the child, the children, who form the groups, not the adult!

One day I was talking to a Montessori elementary student about school in general and I asked how it was different than the primary class he had attended for four years. What he really enjoyed was being able to pick a subject to learn about and not having it assigned. But there was a problem. One day he had approached his Montessori teacher and asked for direction to begin researching a subject. Rather than giving the advice he was seeking, the teacher took him by the hand and said, "Let's go find someone to do this research with you." That was not his plan, and it didn't work out, and he stopped asking this teacher for advice on research.

Sometimes an adult thinks that they need to oversee the arranging the students in groups, maybe so everyone is included, or so the work is balanced, or maybe just because it

is well-known that exploring social groups is part of the age. However, in my experience, children who are happy will never allow someone to be left out; if the work load in a project is not balanced and fair, the students will be the first to point this out and self-correct; and just as we adults would cringe at the very idea of someone else deciding who we should spend our time with, children feel the same.

Forming a group and working together as a group is an important skill, that the children should master on their own.

*Age 6-12 characteristic—learning through the mind rather than only the senses*

In the first six years a child wants to experience, touch,

and then learn the name of everything. Examples might be the items throughout the house, tools and clothing, food, wildflowers, cars, etc.

Around age six things change. Instead of "what" this older child wants to know "why?" and "when?" because the imagination starts to function. Instead of just knowing what grows in the family or school garden, now he wants to know when humans began to plant crops rather than just eating wild plants. How did humans begin to count and why?

*Age 6-12 characteristic—ready for a wider environment for exploration*

In the first six years we speak of "bringing the world into the classroom." But at this new stage we figure out many ways to get the children out into the world. There are many people in every community who have a lot to offer children at this age as they explore society, work, religion, attitudes; and they love to hear the stories of community members.

When I was in 5$^{th}$ grade in public school in our small community the teacher assigned a hands-on project. We were asked to choose between making a butterfly collection or a leaf collection. Not wanting to kill butterflies, I choose the leaf collection. Hearing this my mother introduced me to a man who had collected trees from all over the world that were now full grown and spread all over his large property. The man and I spent hours together; he told me about the country he had visited for each example; how he had brought it back with him; what he had learned about the variation in the needs—light, water, temperature—of each one; and the local and scientific names for each.

I collected one or two leaves from each tree, pressed them, and created an amazing leaf collection. Time spent on this assignment was one of the few educational experiences in my school years that taught me something that lasted throughout life. It is partly responsible for my desire to travel, being constantly aware of nature when I am in a different country and enjoying teaching botany to others.

And my guide for the day? He thought it was wonderful to have a young person so interested in something that was clearly a life-long passion for him. As parents and grandparents, and teachers, we can look for people like this in our own communities.

*Age 6-12 characteristic—being valuable and helpful*

Everyone wants to be needed. Because of the low adult to student ratio in the elementary class, just like in the one-room schoolhouse, children learn how important they are as they form groups to solve problems and even look around for someone to help. Many schools encourage visits between classes to give the elementary (and middle school) students opportunities to help in the younger classes.

*Details of a Montessori elementary class—no grades, no tests*

This is such a fundamental part of Montessori that

sometimes we forget to mention it. There is no need for reward because the work is the reward. There is no comparing of the progress of students of the same age because of the mixed ages in the class. Children choose what to work on, help each other when necessary, and work until they are satisfied with the task, not for someone else's satisfaction. They usually set higher standards for themselves than a teacher would.

When I had students who were in their last year with me and ready to move on to a traditional school, I provided an experience of what it is like to take a test. But we did it in an interesting way. First, I explained why tests are given, why they are necessary when a teacher has a group of students for only one year and sometimes only one hour a day. And how difficult it might be for a traditional teacher who has been told what each of her students should have learned by the end of the years. Then, the students and I prepared the environment, the tables, the correct distance between students so they could not look at others' work, and someone (a younger student who was not taking the test) to watch the clock and tell them when to begin taking the test and when it was over. The tested students themselves graded their tests (that had been given to us by friends in a traditional school). And sometimes they even figured out the concept of grading on a curve. They learned a practical skill and developed confidence.

*Details of a Montessori elementary class——no required homework*

The reason for no assigned homework is that rather than receiving assignments to work on at home, all the work is done during class time. And because of the long work periods, choice of work, and levels of concentration, the work done in class is far more likely to be retained, to be learned.

There are times when a student, or a small group of students, continue working on a project at home. But most of the work is completed during the day.

*Details of the Montessori elementary class—the role of the teacher*

Seldom have I seen a teacher's desk in a Montessori elementary class and I never had one myself. The teacher is not the center, the boss, the assigner of work and schedule. The teacher is the observer and facilitator, striving always to help the students become independent in planning their work, experimenting with learning styles and needs, setting goals and reaching them. She meets weekly with each student, suggesting ways to meet the required work (by the state or country), and for branching out to explore as widely as possible what is available in the environment. Her goal is to eventually enable the student to become independent even of these meetings with the teacher, being able to manage time and reach goals on their own. Just imagine how such skills will benefit a person throughout life.

*Details of a Montessori elementary class—real work of the community*

Sometimes, wanting to leave time for the child's schoolwork, parents offer to do all the real, daily, family work to leave time for the child's academic studies. But it is a good idea to carry out this work together for several reasons: the skills of daily life are important throughout life; contributing to the family through this work helps the child feel needed and valuable. Too often, when a child at this age no longer feels like a contributing member of the family his attention turns to entertaining himself, searching for fleeting pleasure, shopping, "hanging out" with friends, etc. This can begin to create a schism between the child and the family.

Margaret Stephenson, my elementary course teacher trainer, advised us to keep in mind the physical needs of humans—food, clothing, shelter, transportation—from the primary class when thinking about how to involve children in the practical life of the home or school.

*Real work, food*: Using the human need for food as an example of bringing everyday work into the classroom, I know an elementary teacher whose 6-12 students cook and serve lunch once a week. The children plan the menu by looking through the cookbooks in the kitchen of the school, they make a list of foods needed to be purchased and project what the cost will be. They arrange transportation to take them to the grocery store. They look at the quality, and compare prices, of what they are planning to purchase. Upon returning to the school they prepare the meal, set the table, invite the others to eat, wash the dishes and the kitchen, and go back to their individual work.

*Academics— work required by the state or country*

The basic state or country requirements, in math for example, are covered but how this is done is unique for each child. It is made clear what is required at each traditional grade level. The teacher works with each child individually to make a weekly, then bi-weekly or monthly, or yearly plan and shows the student how to experiment with different schedules. When the standards are not met there is no punishment, but a conversation which results in the student figuring out how to get the required work finished.

*Academics—the Montessori curriculum*

Throughout the day each student is free, and encouraged, to follow a unique path.

Here is a quote from Dr. Montessori:

> *The children studied but there was complete freedom in their study, and they could apply themselves to anything they liked. They are completely free to study what they like and the means to do so are given to them*

(Kodaikanal 1942 lecture, from AMI Communications 2011)

The 6-12 curriculum is divided into five areas that, taken together, are known as cosmic education. Throughout the years a child spends in the class, these five areas are woven together in creative ways that give surety that all subjects are interesting and valuable. Here is a short introduction to the five main areas that form the structure of all the academic work, not as isolated subjects but as areas of knowledge that constantly flow from one to the others, inspiring a child to develop an interest in all, through his own research or exposure to the research going on around him by his fellow students.

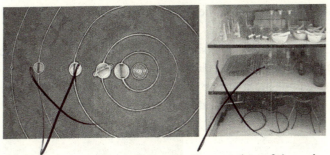

*The first great lesson* presents the creation of the universe and opens the door to the study of astronomy, geology, geography, physics, chemistry, and other areas of study concerning the physical universe and the planet earth. Charts and experiments bring the study into the present.

*The second great lesson* presents the evolution of plants and animals and how they continue to evolve; their needs; how varieties traveled from one continent to another, and much more. The point is to awaken curiosity that inspires research. For example, one of my students learned that the potato traveled from South America to Ireland and was the main staple of food especially for the poor. Then, because of the reliance on only two varieties that became vulnerable to disease, the crops were wiped out and the Irish potato famine of the 1840s was the result. That research taught us, the other students and me, the value of genetic variation to protect food sources.

I once heard of a Montessori student, after the experience of growing food for the class in the school garden, say that she never let one grain of rice go to waste on her plate now that she knew what is involved in growing it.

Another Montessori class story combined the interest of a student in the Jurassic and Cretaceous periods of the evolution timeline with exploration in math. It was told to me by a colleague. His eight-year-old student was excited to share with her friends how the Fibonacci sequence (a sequence in which each element is the sum of the two elements that precede it—creating the spiral often found in nature) is related to the ammonite.

After visiting a museum and seeing and touching an ammonite fossil, and reading the exhibit signage, she learned that they grew to be much larger than she had thought. So, she decided to create a piece of art, drawing and painting a full-size ammonite, to share this amazing fact with her friends.

*The third great lesson*, the study of human history, begins with students imagining what life might have been like for all the years when there was no fire, no growing of crops, what were the first words necessary, did singing come before speaking? A whole world opens for them by studying the physical needs introduced in the primary class (food, clothing, shelter, transportation) and how these were determined by the geography and climate where humans lived.

During my Montessori elementary training and teaching there was no dividing the 6-12 class into two smaller age groupings (6-9 and 9-12) so the suggested exploration of history, based on observations of children's interests was: age 6-7 prehistory and the measurement of time; age 8-9 emphasis on ancient civilizations; age 10-12 human history in "modern" times, including the children's own country and local community history, and biographies of people who have influenced this story.

This is another reason to suggest contacting experts in the community to interview, and trips to museums to satisfy curiosity and answer questions.

In a traditional class the teacher might assign each student to pick a culture and begin to research it. But such adult-directed projects are not Montessori practice; instead, the teacher is looking constantly for a child's interests, listening to his questions, and then providing guidance to an interesting direction by which he can learn more,

For example, along with the physical needs of humans, at this age the student (at home and in class) is naturally interested in mental needs (exploration, language, math, and science) and spiritual needs (vanity, culture, art, religions). There are a series of charts that guide a student who has an interest in a specific culture. Here are examples of questions on each of these four charts:

*The nature of the country*—What were the soil and climate like? What were the flora and fauna like? What people lived there? Where did they come from and why?

*The practical activities of the people*—what were the types of work and occupations? What did they produce? What tools and techniques did they have? How did they find their country and how did they make it more habitable? How did they make use of natural resources?

*The intellectual and spiritual aspects of culture*—What language did they speak? What was the education like? How advanced was their learning? What was their art like? What were their ideas of life and death? Who, if anyone, was the spiritual leader? What concept of justice was there?

*Relations within the group and with other groups*—Did they trade among themselves? Did they trade with others? By barter or other means? What about their wars and conquests? Did they have slaves and take people into subjugation? What about travel and migration? How and why did the group settle where they did? How were their money and goods held? Individually or tribally? What about their dress, food, houses, customs, family life, how were they governed? What care did they give to their children? Was there care taken of the poor?

*An example of history research*

One year I had a student who wanted to research a local Native American group in all the areas presented on these four charts. He went to the library after school hours with his parents to find books and brought them to class. He drew pictures and gathered information in each area and, when he was satisfied with his work, made a presentation to the rest of the class. (Such student presentations are common and are posted ahead of time on the class bulletin board in order for other students to plan their schedules to be present.)

Then he decided to branch out to explore other Native American cultures. There 109 different groups in California alone and he continued this research for months.

Imagine the scene: as he is doing this work, other students in the classroom are each following their own individual path. And just as this knowledge about Native American cultures passively educated each person in the room, whatever the others were studying and creating also influenced our Native American specialist.

*The arts as part of the third great lesson*

Learning about the history and development of the songs and dances, the decoration of clothing, and homes, in the child's own culture, awakens a desire to understand how the arts developed in other places.

In one of the civilization study charts, we see that "The intellectual and spiritual aspects of culture" includes all the arts.

It has been my great pleasure to observe children is a variety of places—Peru, Colombia, Mexico, Bhutan, India, Morrocco, Romania, and Bhutan as examples—where music and dance are part of the curriculum.

One year I was talking to a few of the children in a Montessori elementary class about the kind of music they like. They looked at each other, smiled, and quietly started singing a song taught to them by their teacher. A few of the children next to us joined in and then, very quickly, the whole class exploded into song and dance, leaving their work behind for a moment, clearly expressing the same kind of love for this song that had been modeled by their Montessori teacher! And then just as quickly, returned, each one, to their individual projects.

This is the very best kind of "group activity" found in a Montessori class, because it was spontaneously formed and led by the children.

*The result of the Montessori approach to history*
Later, when these students might be required to learn

world or local history in high school or college, this background on the study of the needs of human beings will have created a different world view. This work might have prepared these students to see all people, no matter what the race, color, gender, religion, as one human family, having much in common with all others on the planet because they understand that we are all trying to satisfy the same needs. This can lead to adults who assign much less blame to others and exhibit more understanding, and hopefully have fewer disagreements and wars, listen to others, and solve problems through dialogue.

*The fourth great lesson* explores human language in all aspects.

Reading books from the school or community library goes on at any time, children reading alone or reading to each other. For children entering a Montessori elementary class who are behind in both reading and writing, I have found that it is a fellow student that can be the best teacher, reading along with the new student, just as his parent did with him in the home as he was learning to read.

*A language research project*

The Montessori "migration" study chart is intended to arouse curiosity and inspire research on why a group of people moved from one place to another. One of my students was very interested in how migrations have affected the spread of languages. I showed him how to look up the languages spoken in France (his choice). Then we took out a large piece of paper and, looking at the globe, he drew an outline of the country. In the lower corner of the paper, he made a little legend assigning each language a color. Together we decided to draw colored lines through the country of France. At first, he was satisfied in just one colored line for each language spoken, but then he decided that since far more people spoke French than the other language, there should be more lines representing the French language than others. This required math. And more colored lines on the outline map of France.

Just as the civilization charts led to research on many Native American cultures, this led to more language research on more countries, more hand-drawing of country outlines, more math, and so on. In this one instance I remember several other students coming to watch who asked me if they could do the same thing.

*Debating*

Sharing opinions and having conversations is a need at this age. One day in my elementary class, two boys were arguing a political point and not getting very far. I approached them and asked if they were interested in carrying out an official debate with their arguments. Of course they were. I asked them to write down all the points they could think of in their favor. The only suggestion I made was that it would be good if the two lists contained the same number of points.

By this time two other students who had overheard what I had suggested joined in. Now there were two people on each side of the argument. When they had listed all the points supporting their argument, I asked them to sit on the floor, as two teams, facing each other and asked if I could join in. At this point several other students had stopped their work and joined us, as a quiet audience. The two sides very politely went through their points, taking turns. Neither side changed their minds, but they had enjoyed being in neutral as they listened to the other person.

Then, I asked if we could do it again but with my participation. They thought this was very funny, but we began. I sat on one side and contributed arguments against the other side whenever I could.

Then? I changed sides.

Now on the opposite side I argued each point. All the students were staring at me with mouths hanging open, and comments along the line of, "But you just said . . . !" (Quoting me when I was arguing on the other side.) and "But what is the truth?" and "Which position is the correct one." And "Who is right?"

I could have offered the use of the talking stick (the person holding the stick speaks until he feels heard, and then passes it on) but I wanted to help them become aware of the fact that people can argue a position for many different reasons, even without believing in it; and it is better to look behind the words and try to understand the reasons for both sides of an argument.

Ideally this lesson stayed with the students as they learned to think and act by themselves and made intelligent decisions about others and the world.

> *Empathy is patiently and sincerely seeing the world through the other person's eyes. It is not learned in school: it is cultivated over a lifetime.* —Albert Einstein

*The fifth great lesson*, explores the concepts and practices of geometry and math and how the need for this information must have developed as groups of humans grew, as they settled into agrarian communities, as their animal herds grew in number, and on and on.

There are interesting facts connected with the development of math just as with language. For example, since English writing goes from left to right, children are very interested to learn that Egyptian writing was determined by the orientation of the human and animal figures in the hieroglyphics, so sometimes it is written from left to right, sometimes right to left, and at times from top to bottom. Also, ancient Egyptians did not have the concept of zero in their math; just try to do some math problems without it. Children love to try.

One year I had a student who became entranced by the Montessori geometry program, materials and booklets containing drawings and definitions of concepts beginning with simple concepts: from a point to a solid, through lines, angles, plane figures, Pythagorean and Euclid theorems, area, solid geometry and volume. There are about 35 of these definition booklets (which we all made ourselves in those years since they were not available commercially).

Over a period of several months this student made her own set of booklets, drawing and coloring in the pictures, writing out the definitions by hand, making covers from thick colored paper, and punching holes to fasten each book together. Her mother told me much later that this was her daughter's best school year of her life. I think it was largely because of this self-initiated geometry project.

When math is approached, not as a stepped curriculum, but as an exciting human creation, each element having come about for a reason, it is a lot more interesting to children. When it is not a requirement that each child master each skill set whether he is interested or not, there is room for incredibly interesting exploration.

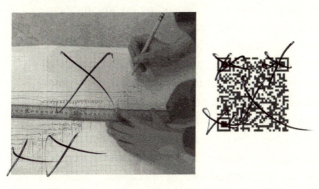

A colleague once shared a video with me of his student who was soon to be celebrating his ninth birthday. To mark this event, the student had decided to divide the largest number that might work, which was one centillion (1 followed by 303 zeros or $10^{303}$), by the number nine. It took many pieces of paper, and a yardstick to keep the rows of figures straight, as the solution went on and on.

This enormous undertaking is a typical example of the Montessori saying, "The teacher is in charge of the minimum, the child is in charge of the maximum."

*Academics—individual and group lessons*

As far as group lessons in my elementary classes, the only scheduled group lessons were the "five great" lessons described above, given at the beginning of each year to introduce the entire curriculum. Other than these, the lessons I gave were mostly 1:1, a lesson given by me to one child, or by a child to another child. The only exception would be when a group of students had formed spontaneously to work on something and came to me to join them because they had some questions.

One day I decided to try a scheduled group lesson. There were four children in my class who were at different stages in the Montessori square root work that contains between eight to fourteen steps or passages, depending on how they are classified, and that are spread out usually over weeks. Since these four were all deeply involved in work, alone or with others, I did not interrupt them. Over lunch I suggested my plan and asked them to, if interested, decide on a time convenient to all of them and let me know, which they did.

During that square root group lesson the value of 1:1 lessons became even more clear to me. We had a good time together, and they enjoyed the experiment, but I could easily tell that they were understanding my demonstration at different speeds, and I had to adjust my lesson to be sure that the slowest person understood, causing the others to sit and wait.

Just as is explained at the beginning of this chapter, one of the benefits of mixed ages in the Montessori elementary class is that by the time an individual lesson ends, the teacher can be pretty sure that the information has been taken in. And as the student repeats the work, then gives this 1:1 lesson to a peer, the learning becomes even more solid, more part of the neural connections in the brain. These students make excellent teachers of others.

*My own learning, and learning at home*

Over the years I have thought a lot about group and 1:1 learning, and why individual lessons are such an important part of Montessori education over the years. I think back on the times during which I really learned something and retained the information—making noodles with my grandmother, individual music lessons, gardening with my father, practicing lessons with other adults during Montessori teacher training. My true learning almost always occurred during time with one person.

Human beings began farming about 12,000 years ago, but even before that, during the hunter-gatherer years, and later when private tutors teaching children at home was the only possibility, children learned mostly through 1:1 lessons from adults. This is the natural way. And it is the natural way for parents and grandparents, and a supportive community, to contribute to the education of children at this age.

In many years as a Montessori school consultant, I have seen in classes where individual-lessons are standard practice, the atmosphere is calm, and quiet, the children satisfied with their work, confident to continue along their individual paths, kind, and exhibiting a desire to help others.

I end this chapter with two quotes from a colleague, John McNamara, an inspiring and experienced teacher, consultant, and speaker.

One of the joys of being part of the Montessori community of parents and teachers, is that we know we will never have all the answers, and we continue to be there for each other during this world-wide movement.

This quote is from the book *Please Help Me Do It Myself, Observation and Recordkeeping for the Montessori Primary and Elementary Class*:

*The only lessons that I give to the whole class are the Great Lessons. Less is more when it comes to lessons. I don't know how many times a student has gotten upset at me when I attempted to interrupt the student in order to give a lesson. I am still learning.*

*I really believe that over-emphasis on curriculum causes the stress and causes the teachers to ask themselves the question, "How can I get the students to do what I want?" (cover the curriculum) instead of more important questions. For example,*

*-What do my students need?*

*-How can I meet these needs?*

*-Under what conditions are students most likely to feel that they can be successful?*

*-When are students most likely to become curious?*

*Teachers have to observe their students more and observe when they are truly engaged because:*

*A busy student is not necessarily an engaged student.*

And from *The Secret of Childhood*:

*When because of favorable circumstances work flows naturally from an inner impulse, it assumes an entirely different character, even in adults. When this happens, work becomes fascinating and irresistible and raises a man above his diverted self. Examples of this may be found in the toils of an inventor, the discoveries of explorers, and the paintings of artists.*

# AGE TWELVE TO EIGHTEEN YEARS

Young adults need our understanding, care, and support, in the 21$^{st}$ century more than ever before. They continually hear bad news: the environment, the cost of college loans and houses, and more. And above all they are learning that the professions open to their parents might be obsolete by the time they are adults—so why work so hard and spend so much time on traditional subjects preparing for a world that will be so different from now?

The Montessori program for this age is vastly different from what was considered a good middle and high school education in the past. It is focused on physical, mental, and social aspects of human development. And when these needs are met, students are confident in themselves, patient and kind to each other, happy, and filled with curiosity and a passion to think independently, solve problems, and learn more.

*Sweden*

In the fall of 2018, I arrived at The Montessori Center for Work and Study boarding school on a working farm in Sweden, put my suitcase in a little guest cabin that had been built by the students and staff, and joined one of the young men who was cleaning the kitchen.

The next morning, still dark, I was invited to join one of the students who was cleaning the barn and feeding the cows. Later in the day adults began arriving from around Europe for the Adolescent teacher education program. They had been together here previously, living and learning with the students in an intensive course on Montessori theory and practice for this age. They had returned home to implement these ideas with their own adolescent students, and were now reporting on what they had attempted, their failures and successes, and perhaps inspire each other to go back and do even more. I was only invited to speak because of my varied experienced with this age group and was thrilled to hear their reports of what these teachers and their young adult students were doing.

The students at this school oversee much of the practical work which helps them become physically and emotionally strong, very important especially in the first years of this fragile age, when so many changes are going on in the body and the brain. The physical work is the same as if they were adults, and it provides a feeling of being useful, and of value to the community.

They grow as much of their own food as possible and freeze or can for the winter and to sell in the community; they cook and clean and take care of the farm and each other and still maintain high academic standards.

Because of the many guests who want to come to visit the farm school in Sweden, and the lack of places for them to stay, the students and teachers worked together to build guest houses. And the students took on the responsibility for feeding and hosting the guests.

*The 12-18 Environment*

*Farm school:* Dr. Montessori called the ideal environment for this age an Erdkinder, a German word that means earth children. There were many reasons for this including being out in the fresh air, doing real work, becoming aware of one's value as a contributing member of a society, and much more. When planning the building for a stand-alone program like this one it is best to think of it as a home, not a school. There are no "Montessori materials" such as are found in programs for younger students. The Montessori materials are the adults—not only their adult teachers but adults that represent different roles in society.

There are a few full-time boarding schools like this, but they are rare for several reasons. Montessori residential communities, like all boarding schools, are expensive and some only survive because of generous donations. As a result, they are only available to a few. It is very important that such experimental schools exist because this is a true scientific laboratory where parents and educators can learn about the developmental needs, and the possibilities for human attainment, creativity, and happiness, at this age.

*Programs in cities*: Many 12-18 Montessori environments exist in a city and are part of a large Montessori school; often with periodic experiences in the countryside. An advantage is that these young adults can tutor, and help in other ways, the younger children, those in the infant communities, primary classes, and elementary. This teaches adolescents not only the value of the academics they have learned, but life skills, and more information about themselves, and sometimes inspiration for professions.

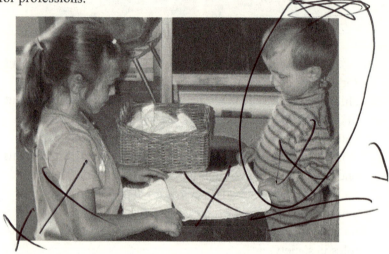

One of the disadvantages of programs in the cities is when a person who is in the process of becoming an adult and going through the rapid physical and emotional changes of this age—and living at home—there is great demand on parents to understand the changes and needs, and to keep up with their children: *Am I reverting to the authoritarian way I was treated? Am I treating this young adult as though he were eight years old? Do I have old expectations in my mind that keep me from seeing him right now? Can I listen carefully and learn from my child just as he has learned from me over the years? Can I let go and trust instead of controlling and advising? I see that he is very different than he was a few months ago, and I look forward to what comes next. How can I*

*learn to let go and let my child learn to meet responsibilities and solve problems on his own?*

Parents with the time and interest to do so, can develop the same kind of observation skills as the Montessori teacher, learning from the constantly changing young adult, and in the process learning more about themselves and the definition of a well-lived life.

*Montessori adolescent teacher education courses*

Montessori teacher courses at this level are attended not only by Montessori teachers, but by traditional teachers, and others interested in these ideas and practices. Traditional teachers, depending on the support of their administration and others, have implemented much of what they learn on the courses. The 25-hour *adolescent orientation course* is held online. The *adolescent diploma course* is much longer and at least partially in person.

I had been invited to join this final session of the much longer Montessori 12-18 diploma course in Sweden to share some of my own experiences with this age group—Latin tutor, counselor for girls in prison, homeschooler, Montessori 0-3 experience that is of interest to the young adolescent, and parent. But I came away wishing that I had known everything I learned in Sweden this week before carrying out my other work with adolescents. Here is some of what they taught me.

The environment for adolescent students is not called a school, but "a center for study and work." This is for ages 12-18. The first two years should be considered a vacation from academics because of all the changes going on in this child's brain and body. There should ideally be the time to focus on rest and physical strength.

This is more likely to be possible if the students previously attended a Montessori 6-12 class or parents and teachers were aware of the needs of that stage of life. These earlier six years are the time when children ask the big questions such as "What happened to the dinosaurs? Who discovered geometry? Why are there so many languages on earth?" etc. It is a time of steady and gradual physical and emotional growth (unlike age 0-6 and 12-18!). They easily focus on intellectual pursuits, and much of the academic work that usually would be part of a middle school (or beginning of secondary school) program are covered. Emphasis then can be on society, figuring out "who I am" and experimenting with different skills.

*The academic curriculum.*

The idea of *cosmic education* (interconnectedness of all fields of knowledge and search for one's unique role in this scheme) is prepared for in the primary class through the hands-on activities in the arts and sciences, history and geography. At the 6-12 level this preparation is pulled together in what is called the *five great lessons* discussed earlier in this book. These five areas are kept in mind when offering work at the 12-18 level.

Even though—just as at the 6-12 level—students have support for their choice of study, and a student might spend weeks or months focusing on only one or two areas, each student will be aware that colleagues are following different paths of exploration, research, and mastery. This awareness of the passion and work of colleagues is a continual reminder that all areas of study and expertise are interesting and valuable; it provides daily practice in communicating from different perspectives, enriching all. Wonderful preparation for life.

*The schedule*

A friend of mine is a well-known psychologist doing very important research on outcomes, academic, emotional, and social, of Montessori experience compared to other forms of education. I will share her wisdom again, as I did in the last chapter.

> *Traditional schooling is forever in turmoil because of its poor ideological foundation. First, traditional schools are modeled on factories, because the birth of mass public schooling coincided with the age of efficiency. Efficiency is a laudable goal, but it led to the creation of a school system that treats children as if they were all pretty much the same. In some ways they are, but in many ways, they are not, and the factory model has a host of consequences that result in sub optimal learning conditions. We might also question its relevance to today's social and economic conditions in which individual initiative, rather than blind obedience to the bells of a factory, is the key to progress.*
>
> —Dr. Angeline Lillard, author of *Montessori, the Science Behind the Genius:*

A regularly scheduled 50-minute class system is seldom found in Montessori adolescent programs unless a student is taking a class at a local junior college or university, or if it is necessary to accommodate a visiting lecturer requested by the students. Unless the class is the result of a student interest and request this is an inefficient way to learn.

The following quote is from *Montessori and Mindfulness* (the chapter "Flow, the Secret of Happiness"):

*Here is an example of an experiment with high school students in China. Each student was given a pager programmed to go off at 10 unpredictable times during a school day. Each time the pager sounded, the students were instructed to identify what they were doing, what they were thinking about, and how they are feeling.*

*The teacher was giving a very interesting and entertaining whole-group lesson on the Genghis Khan. As the students' pagers went off during the lesson this is what the students recorded as their thoughts:*

*Of 27 students in the class, 25 didn't mention anything vaguely connected with China; they mentioned their dates, their coming football game, how hungry they were, how sleepy they were, etc. There were 2 who mentioned China but nothing about the Genghis Khan.*

*The daily work, together and the individual path*

In Montessori 12-18 environments there are many opportunities for creative problem-solving and creative work, independently or collaborating with other students and adults. On a farm-school or residential community, it is easy for each student to feel valuable and bit-by-bit to improve their skills in different areas and feel needed by the community. And providing such opportunities is the challenge for part-time or city adolescent Montessori programs. In setting up such an environment, the adults and students work together; the attitude is rather like setting up one's own home, creating ways for the adolescents to be (as much as possible) in charge of the cleaning, the maintenance, decorating, planning menus, shopping and cooking, overseeing the budget and money

This is an area that can be brought into the home, the parents and young adults working together to plan. This can help balance peer pressure to be a certain way and can help an individual find a unique path.

*Combining the practical and the academic*

In Montessori at this age there is a combination of the practical skills necessary to develop the responsibility and the problem-solving ability needed to care for a family with the physical and mental skills that lead to mastery of a profession. In both areas adaptability is essential because of the rapidly changing present and future.

In the world there are many situations where people are trying to implement Montessori practice for this age. In some communities, such as in cities, there is an emphasis of the academic with no practical experience in important daily living. In smaller, farm-type communities, there is plenty of practical experience but there is often a lack of the academic skills that will be needed in the future no matter where a young person lives.

Here are some examples of practical work combined with academics from different Montessori 12-18 programs around the world. Such projects are not limited to Montessori schools but can inspire family projects as well.

*India*

The intention, and the situation in many examples around the world today, is a successful combination of the practical and the academic. As in all Montessori 12-18 programs around the world, the academics is not a set curriculum that is prescribed by adults but grows out of the real work and spontaneous inspiration inspired by often unexpected experiences and interests. Here are some examples:

What began as gardening to provide the food for those at a farm school in India, became a study of farming in India, plant varieties, famines, and the importance of creating a seed bank to preserve as many varieties as possible in case they are needed in the future. At the same school the student became interested in life along the rivers, and the health of rivers, and set out to learn as much as possible in this field of knowledge. Students each year chose three main projects, such as cocoa production and grafting and other farming techniques, and all their academic and practical work were connected.

*Colombia*

In a school in Colombia the students make toiletries packages, gather blankets and clothes from the community, cook food, and deliver all to homeless people in the center of the city. One of the homeless men, grateful for their help, told the students, *Montessori is a very good method. I was a university teacher, and the drugs have me in the street.*

Conversations with these people provide unique and valuable insight, and the teachers report that they inspire students to work hard at developing their skills and knowledge to be the kind of adult that will help alleviate such hopeless life situations.

*The United States*

In a school here in the US there are students from several countries, some from cold and some from hot countries. Here they learn how to do the practical work, such as tapping the maple sugar trees in the winter to make maple syrup and following the seasons for growing a garden and crops.

Some of the students who were independently studying Spanish volunteer to work with the local Spanish speaking schoolchildren on reading English. They serve meals at a shelter for the homeless, and research regional and global challenges like clean water and food access.

*Mexico*

At one of the oldest Montessori schools in the country the staff prepare the meals in the school restaurant for Monday and Tuesday each week, and the students—who have been involved with the school gardening and raising of farm animals—plan the meals, shop for food needed from stores, do the cooking, care for the school restaurant and serve food for the rest of the week.

*Granja Hogar* (beautiful place) is a non-profit organization that has been run by Sacred Heart, a Catholic organization, for many years. It provides clothing and supplies for families, and farming and gardening experience and academic education for the disadvantaged Tarahumara children living in the poorest neighborhoods in Chihuahua. The children stay here from Sunday night through Friday.

Some years ago, adolescent students from the Montessori school began spending time each week working on this farm, participating in building maintenance, caring for the children, and helping with education. Eventually these volunteer Montessori students requested that the Montessori school create a Montessori preschool for these children.

Today the school provides the materials and the teachers to give the best of Montessori to the poorest of Chihuahua, changing the lives of not only these children and their families, but also everyone involved with the Montessori school.

### A school in the Caribbean

In my class in an old sugar plantation on St. Croix (ages 6-15 out of necessity) class there were two 13-year-olds who were behind academically and spent every spare moment talking about skateboarding. They wanted to own and manage a skateboard store and build a local skateboard park. The attitude toward all their schoolwork was to get it finished quickly and get back to their passion. This was an important goal, so I asked them some questions to get them thinking about what they could learn now that would prepare them for their dream.

They began to interview business owners to learn the cost of retail space, the wholesale cost of skateboards, the profit margin. They interviewed their parents to learn about the cost of rent or house payments, food, clothing, transportation. They wanted to know how much an adult had to earn to afford life on the US Virgin Island where we lived. They researched everything related to managing money, starting a business, purchasing land and so on. They became passionate learners, and the subjects of their research grew considerably. Two noticeable changes occurred: in their interviews with their parents and retail business owners they began to feel respected as adults; the academic work in the classroom took on a new meaning and was approached as valuable study for their skateboarding future.

*Work in our home*

Having lived in many cities around the world it is a pleasure for my husband and me to live here on the north coast of California. We designed our home and did some work in creating it. Our favorite pastime is going for walks and gardening. It is an inspiring place for me to write (first the Michael Olaf Montessori catalogues for the company run my husband, and subsequently, books like the one you are reading.)

Having spent many years designing and creating Montessori environments for children of different ages it was the same here. Our oldest grandchild is 25 years old, but she, and her brother and cousins have spent as much time as possible here, welcomed with a lot of real, practical work such as harvesting berries and potatoes, hauling and stacking the winter firewood, cooking and planning family meals.

You might find, in your role as parent or other educator, that once you enter the world of carefully observing children and young adults, figuring out what they need, attempting to meet their needs and spark their curiosity, that your life will be enriched in ways you never imagined.

*Concentration, time to process, sleep*

During each day of the Montessori experience, from birth on, the Montessori adult is aware of the value of deep concentration. At this 12-18 level, if the students are working on real and practical projects, or academic research projects, they learn to pay attention to their health, and to respect the concentration of others.

I am going to share here one of my favorite quotes, referring to young children, but true for adolescents and us adults:

> *When the children had completed an absorbing bit of work, they appeared rested and deeply pleased. It almost seemed as if a road had opened up within their souls that led to all their latent powers, revealing the better part of themselves. They exhibited a great affability to everyone, put themselves out to help others and seemed full of good will.*
>
> *It was clear to me that the concept of order and the development of character, of the intellectual and emotional life, must derive from this veiled source. Thereafter, I set out to find experimental objects that would make this concentration possible, and carefully worked out an environment that would present the most favorable external conditions for this concentration. And that is how my method began.*
>
> —Montessori, *The Child in the Family*

Each of us has figured out our own method of reaching a place of calm, where we can process our day perhaps, and prepare to be patient and kind to those around us. It might be meditation, prayer, singing, gardening. In Montessori teaching it is always in our mind to watch for the same for our children.

Young adults need time to process what they are learning, to stop and think, to discuss with others, to experiment. These individuals have different needs, some learning more by discussion some by being alone and thinking. Some might need to walk in nature as did this great thinker:

> *Einstein's daily walk was sacred to him. While he was working at Princeton University, New Jersey, he'd walk the mile and a half journey there and back. He followed the practice of other walkers, including Darwin who went for three 45-minute walks every day. These walks were not just for health. We know today that there is a lot of evidence that walking can boost memory, creativity and problem solving.*
>
> — Stephenson, *Montessori and Mindfulness* (the chapter "Mindfulness, Support and Impediments")

One sometimes hears that adolescents need to sleep longer in the morning and some schools accommodate this by starting high school classes later. But over the years I have observed traditionally schooled students whose "school" day begins at 8 or 9 in the morning and goes until 8 or 9PM, completely taken up by schooltime and homework; as a result, the only time they must process life, to think and communicate with their friends (now usually on phones) is late at night. The natural result is, of course, that they will need to sleep late in the morning.

There is a lot of talk about the impulsivity and immaturity of the teen brain, but when the adolescent has physical, mental, and emotional support in this rapidly changing time of life, his brain has an amazing ability to adapt and respond to new experiences and situations. Taking challenging classes, exercising, and engaging in creative activities like art or music can strengthen brain circuits and help the brain mature. We now know that changes to the areas of the brain responsible for social processes can lead teens to focus more on peer relationships and social experiences, not only outside the home, but in the family.

It is exciting to see the interesting and unique persons emerge during this extremely creative time of life. It is well-known that studying (often cramming) only for a good grade does not remain stored in the brain. So, just as in the early years, a student having the possibility to choose what to study is very important. Independently intentioned research can require consultation with adults not connected to the home or school. Experts can be found out to guide students in their work and research, and this is usually very welcome as anyone is pleased to be asked questions by teenagers who pay attention and make notes.

*Adapting to traditional school after Montessori*

I am going to share some personal stories of our family over the years. Our eldest daughter had attended Montessori preschool and one year of elementary (age 6-12) when she entered a traditional public school in a new town. The administration and the teachers were devoted and doing their best and very interested in having their very first "Montessori student." She had two experiences worth mentioning.

Early in the year she came home with her first textbook (they are not used in Montessori). The assignment was to read a certain chapter. At the end of the chapter there was a section called "extra work" or something like that. In it were suggestions for hands-on activities like those she was used to. Perhaps cooking, exploration of the environment, further reading, art. She spent the evening doing every single one of these suggested activities and took them with her to school the next day, as she thought she was expected to do. But she was disappointed when the teacher kindly explained to her that she should ignore that part of the chapters from then on and just read and try to remember the text.

A few weeks into that semester she brought home her first ever report card. Grades are not part of Montessori, and we had never discussed them. Her grades were not very good, but she did not seem to notice and just casually handed her report card to us and continued her day. We didn't know what to say and discussed it. Finally, I told her that although grades were arbitrary and not very important to us, there might come a time in the future, when perhaps she wanted to go to university or pursue other professional training where acceptance into a program would depend on grades——high grades thought to be indicative of how hard a person works in meeting academic responsibilities—high grades would be better than low. She figured out how to meet the standards set by her teachers and did just fine from then on.

Her sister attended Montessori from age two to twelve years and then attended a public-school arts magnet school where all the academic work was combined with art, everything creative and hands-on and unique. Then she moved to a traditional public high school. Again, very wonderful school and teachers. But she came home after a few days and reported,

"We are supposed to listen to the teacher, or read the book, and then answer questions based on what we just heard or read. What kind of education is that!"

And one last story. I will quote from the book *Montessori Homeschooling, One Family's Story* (page 110):

### The First Test

*Many of Michael's friends attended public school and he often heard them worrying about an upcoming test, something outside of his educational experience until, in a class on music theory at the Saturday Music Academy, he was given a test.*

*That evening as we were having dinner he said:*

*"I don't see what the big deal is about tests. My friends who go to school are always worrying about them. The music test today was no problem. If I didn't know the answer to a question, I just looked at the test of the person sitting next to me."*

*We had to laugh and were able to explain the concept of "cheating." Michael was used to working with, not competing against, others to solve problems. This was his first experience of being asked to give information completely on his own, where his answers would be marked right or wrong by someone else, and then he might be given a grade compared to the grades earned by the other students in the class.*

*We explained that a test could be seen as a way to find out if a teacher was successfully imparting knowledge, and to assess the progress of a student and then give direction where he should focus his energy and time in order to improve. We explained the traditional testing situation in a positive way, but it gave us a lot to think about.*

### College or university classes

There are many examples of students in Montessori adolescent programs taking university level courses to follow their interests. I remember hearing about a Montessori teacher of children in the primary, age 3-6, being asked some questions about the physics experiments she had provided the students. Because she knew she could not answer sufficiently, she invited a professor of physics to visit and explain to the children.

In the 6-12 age there is a part of the curriculum called "going out" where the children themselves plan excursions or invite specialists to help in their research. Since making a weekly plan helps students at this age become capable at planning and reaching their goals, it is possible for those interested in studying a foreign language, or any other subject, to reach out into the community and find mentors or teachers.

It is possible to schedule language classes in some situations, to learn through books and technical aids, but, just as all other academic pursuits, such classes should not be scheduled and assigned by the teacher, they should not come at the expense of the individual choice, deep concentration on self-chosen work, and the unique development of each person.

### Sports

Today we humans get much less exercise than in the past—we drive or are driven rather than walking; we spend hours a day in front of the TV; and become addicted to our phones. We adults can learn to balance this by going to the gym or scheduling exercise, but it is better to provide the possibility for children to develop a balance of being still and moving from a young age.

There is an international teacher-education program called *Montessori sports*—a program aligned with The Association Montessori Internationale (AMI). It begins at the preschool level and goes through high school. I do not have personal experience with this program, but I have heard high praise from all directions. Just as with the *adolescent courses* for adults, Montessori sports courses are open to parents, traditional teachers, coaches, anyone interested in more collaboration and fairness and enjoyment in exercise.

Traditional sports programs usually focus on competition and skill-building alone but, just as in academic subjects, Montessori sports focuses on physical, emotional, and social growth while fostering independence, respect and collaboration. Montessori sports isn't about eliminating competition it's about refining and redefining it. The program offers tools to facilitate healthy competition leadership skills and teamwork. It complements competitive sports by fostering a mindset of self-improvement and respect for others. Just as in the Montessori classroom—because of the wide age-span that results in a wide variety of skills and abilities in one group—the program is designed to create level playing fields, ensuring all children, regardless of age, ability, or experience, feel valued and supported

*Respect*

In all areas of education for all ages, respect is an action, not just a feeling. From the very first days and months of life, in Montessori environments children are spoken to by the adult with a voice that is respectful—no babytalk or limited vocabulary. Even the youngest child will notice and seemingly approve of being spoken to this way. Throughout Montessori primary and elementary classes, they become very used to being spoken to by the adult as though their thoughts and words mattered. But this is not always the case. I have met many adults who truly think they are showing respect for children and young adults, but the message received by their words and voice is not one of respect.

One year I was consulting with two Montessori teachers working with young adults aged 12-18. In our discussions it became clear as we spoke that, although they trusted, respected, and deeply cared for their students, "respecting" them, in theory, they spoke to them in a such way that students did not feel respected; they spoke in the traditional adult-as-expert voice that most of us experienced when we were young; the words, the tone of voice, that of a superior person speaking to an inferior, rather than an equal, human being.

The only way I could make that clear was to speak to them in the same kind of condescending and bossy way that they might use, even though they thought they were respecting their students. Then they got it! Later I contacted these teachers to see if our discussion had an effect. Here was the response of one of the teachers, as recorded in the book *Montessori Homeschooling, One Family's Story*:

> *For me it changed my way of relating to students. I started talking to them as I would another older person and trying to interest them in things the way I would another peer. I would say, "I read an interesting book about Lewis and Clark and was fascinated by . . ." And next thing the child was interested too. It helped me watch for and pull out their interests.*
>
> *It also changed the way of talking to students when they were being too loud, for example. I recall being out to dinner with my parents once and becoming loud and excited until finally a waitress came over and said, "Sorry but your table is being loud, and that table said they are having a hard time hearing each other talk." Everyone laughed and we quieted down. The waitress didn't come over and say, "You are being too loud; you need to be quiet. Or you will have to separate. This is one warning..." Your example came to mind.*
>
> *I began to see how ridiculous it was to talk to people like that. If I said, "We are doing some work over here and can't hear each other because it is loud" the students would fix it without my saying anything else.*
>
> *Yours was a life-shifting lesson for me. And has allowed me to have good relations with young people over the years.*

There are many devoted teachers in traditional and experimental classrooms at this age who want to do the best for their students, but I hear from many that they are very limited in what they can offer young adults because the focus is academics, grades, competing instead of collaborating, getting through the work as quickly as possible and getting into a university. There is neither time nor freedom to attend to the physical and emotional needs of this age. But just maybe small changes can make a difference.

> *The teachers must have the greatest respect for the young personality, realizing that in the soul of the adolescent great values are hidden, and that in the minds of these boys and girls there lies all our hope of future progress and the judgement of ourselves and our times.*
>
> —Montessori, *From Childhood to Adolescence*

# CONCLUSION

This book was created with the aid of many people in order to help parents, grandparents, and educators of all kinds, to understand the growing human being, and find family and community-friendly methods to support this development.

I hope that there are ideas within these pages that will make your journey together as a family, community, and school, successful and enjoyable for all. It is hoped that what Montessori dreamed of so long ago, the revelation of a new kind of human being, will be the result.

> *Times have changed, and science has made great progress, and so has our work; but our principles have only been confirmed, and along with them our conviction that mankind can hope for a solution to its problems, among which the most urgent are those of peace and unity, only by turning its attention and energies to the discovery of the child and to the development of the great potentialities of the human personality in the course of its formation.*
>
> —Montessori, *The Discovery of the Child,*

# MARIA MONTESSORI

*Maria's wise mother*

Throughout this book there are many examples of the main principles of Montessori, including the value of observing children to discover their interests, trusting their choices, encouraging them to solve problems and to think and act for themselves.

Renilde Montessori supported her daughter Maria even when her path veered far from the expected life of a young, educated woman in Italy at that time. Maria's interests over the years included (at secondary school level) studying physics, mathematics and natural sciences, and then graduating from medical school. Later, her changing experiences in the community led to more studies and degrees, and working as a university lecturer in the fields of education, experimental psychology, anthropology, and biology. All her work was based on her own observations and experience and a desire to help those in need, adults as well as children. Renilde Montessori was an example for us, providing the courage to support and trust our children and students in the same way.

*Childhood*

The name "Montessori" has become widespread in education fields, but just who was this person? Understanding a bit of her story will help us understand why her discoveries are important to families and communities today.

Maria Tecla Artemisia Montessori was born and spent the first five years of her life in the small village of Chiaravalle, Italy, in 1870. Travel was done by horse and cart, shopping was done in an outside market, and very few children went to school; instead, they helped with the family work. Renilde

Stoppani, Maria's mother, was a well-educated teacher at the company daycare for the children of employees at the tobacco factory where Maria Montessori's father worked. Renilde had a passion for reading and for helping others. She taught Maria to knit and encouraged her to knit for the poor every day. This helped Maria realize her value as a human being, and to act on a natural compassion for others at a young age.

Maria asked a lot of questions which her parents thought was a sign of intelligence. Her father encouraged her to think about being a teacher and her mother seemed more interested in observing her interests and supporting her choices of what to study throughout her childhood and young adulthood.

*School*

When she was five years old the family moved to an apartment in Rome because of her father's work. Being an only child, Maria enjoyed the city because there were many other children in her life there. At age six she started school. Even though the classroom was cold, and students were required to sit still on hard benches listening to someone talk, she knew she was lucky to be there because she wanted to learn as much as possible. After third grade boys and girls were separated and she went to a girls' school till age twelve. After graduating from this program, the girls were expected to stay home and learn to become proper ladies, good at running a home. This is what her father expected Maria would do.

But Maria wanted to continue to learn outside the home. The only choice was a boys' technical school; she and her mother convinced her father to let her do this.

Maria and one other girl were accepted to attend the boys' technical school but were not allowed to eat lunch with the boys, or to talk to them during recess.

*Medical School*

When she finished this program, she decided to go to medical school! Her father was angry and refused, but she did not give up her dream. Later she applied to medical school but was rejected so she went to speak to the Pope, the head of the Catholic church, and explained her dream. She was allowed to enter medical school as a result. Again, there were special rules such as not being allowed to cut up dead bodies when the male students were engaged in this work during the day; she had to work at night, using candles or oil lamps for light and having no one to talk to when she had questions. She became one of the first women to obtain a Doctor of Medicine degree from the University of Rome. Her dissertation was in neurology which may help explain why research in neuroscience today is so in line with her ideas and practices.

*Inspired by a child*

I will share a story that many think is important. One very discouraging evening during her medical training, Maria went for a walk. And a strange thing happened. She saw a child who was being carried by the mother, but who was intent on manipulating a piece of red paper. Maria followed them and continued to watch the child's interest and concentration on this simple object. She regained her courage and decided to continue with medical school. Many think that this was providential, and a first example of what she over and over told adults to do, "Follow the child."

*Work*

In her first job with a hospital, she visited insane asylums where children who were considered uneducable were also housed since their families did not know what to do with them.

The story of what happened next is widespread, and her work with them well-known. Essentially, she went "back to school" on her own, studying earlier educators who had been successful in educating deaf children. Because such children could not be expected to learn by listening to a teacher speak, they had developed materials for the children to manipulate and learn from. She visited the program in France and then returned home to make similar materials and use them with the "uneducable" children.

The results were so successful that she went back to school to study anthropology and began observing and researching teaching methods to learn as much as she could about the traditional methods of education at the time. She wanted to apply her methods, based more on movement and experience with the senses rather than sitting still and listening to a teacher in a traditional school setting. But it was not possible to experiment in this way with what we might call "typical" children.

*Casa dei Bambini*

In 1906 however, when Montessori was a lecturer in anthropology at the university of Rome, she was contacted to help with a project in a poor district of Rome called San Lorenzo. New apartment buildings had been built by the government to house families living in poverty, but a group of children under six years of age were running wild and defacing the walls of new buildings while their parents were at work. It was decided that it would be less expensive to find someone to create a daycare for these children, than to keep repairing the buildings.

This was Montessori's opportunity.

The first *Casa de Bambini* was created to feed, care for, and entertain this group of children. Toys were donated by her friends and a young woman from San Lorenzo who was completely untrained as a teacher was put in charge of them.

Montessori spent many hours each day observing children in this first daycare setting, going over her notes at night, studying, thinking, and designing a way for the woman in charge to try to implement her everchanging experimental ideas.

This cycle—observe, contemplate, study, contemplate, experiment—continued day after day, just as it does today in Montessori schools.

Completely unexpectedly, over the weeks and months, the children became so independent, self-directing, creative, kind and helpful—because of her experiments—that people came from all over the world to observe for themselves if these reported miracles were true. At times even Montessori herself doubted what she was hearing and seeing. Here are her words describing this period, from the book *The Secret of Childhood* (1946):

> *It took a long time for me to convince myself that this was not an allusion. After each new experience proving such a truth, I said to myself, "I won't believe it yet. I'll believe it next time." Thus, for a long time I remained incredulous, and at the same time deeply stirred and anxious. How many times did I not reprove the children's teacher when she told me what the children had done of themselves? "The only thing that impresses me is the truth." I would reply severely. And I remember that the teacher answered, without taking offence, and often moved to tears: "You are right. When I see*

*such things, I think it must be holy angels who are inspiring these children."*

The details of this experiment, and what followed over the years, are recorded in many places. There is not a country in the world where the name *Montessori* is not known in education circles. But because this chapter is intended to show what a person can do when supported as a young child that is all I am going to share about the story of Maria Montessori.

I encourage that you learn more when the time is right for you. To this end, here is information from the AMI website, and are two recent books that I can recommend.

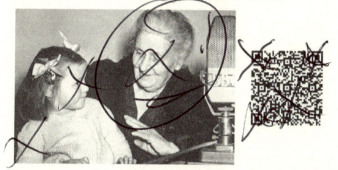

*The Child is the Teacher* (2020) by Cristina de Stefano

This is a very readable story of determination, setbacks, sorrow, and overwhelming success, including information from Montessori's unpublished diaries and letters.

*The Best Weapon for Peace* (2021) by Erica Moretti. This is a thorough examination of Montessori's life-long work, including her push for the creation of the White Cross, a humanitarian organization for war-affected children, and her work with Anna Freud and others. We see how Montessori's educational theories and practices would come to define children's rights, even adopted by the United Nations.

# BOOKS IN THIS SERIES

### *Aid to Life, Montessori Beyond the Classroom*
An experience of teaching "Montessori" in a private girls' school in Peru with no Montessori materials; a newspaper column; homeschooling experiences for age 6-19; Montessori help in Nepal, Tibet, Sikkim, Russia, Morocco: EsF (Educateurs sans Frontieres) Thailand: ideas for the home for ages 0-18; a grandparenting literary experience; observation of a typical day in a Montessori primary class (age 2.5-6.5) in London.

### *Beginnings, Montessori Birth to Three Comparison with Traditions in Bhutan*
Welcomed by new parents-to-be who are overwhelmed by parenting advice because here they can compare two well-tested parenting methods and decide what aligns with their own hopes.

### *Child of the World:*
### *Montessori, Global Education for Age 3-12+*
A brief overview of theory and practice in the Montessori primary, age 2.5-6.5 classroom. The same for the elementary class for ages 6-12. Other chapters: stages of development; the young adult; the adult; preparing the environment; parenting and teaching

### *Glimpses of Aged Care through a Montessori Lens*
Created by Anne Kelly, head of the AMI Montessori for Dementia, Disability, and Ageing training program, and Susan Mayclin Stephenson. They share their unique and complimentary experiences and attitudes toward the last stage of life. This book is enlightening and helpful in cultures where discussions of old age and death are avoided and, as a result, there is little or no preparation.

### *Montessori and Mindfulness*
When practiced authentically, Montessori students spend most of the day being mindful and in the moment. External mindful practices, valuable in other situations, would get in the way. Chapters

include: support and impediments of mindfulness; flow; mindful work, walking, music, exploration; born to be good, and a chapter on mindfulness contributed by the psychologist Dr. Angeline Lillard.

### *Montessori Cosmic Education,*
### *The Child's Discovery of a Global Vision and a Cosmic Task*

A brief introduction to a main Montessori education purpose, which is learning about the world and the interconnectedness of all life, and the search for, and discovery of, one's unique contribution to the world. Ideas for birth through 6-12 years of age are presented.

### *Montessori Homeschooling*

This documentation of a homeschool experiment through elementary, middle, and high school is an inspiration to parents and teachers with only traditional education experience who hope for something more practical, enjoyable, and successful for their children and students.

### *No Checkmate, Montessori Chess lessons for Age 3-90+*

A Montessori way of teaching chess is just one example of how to follow a child's interest and stage of development when teaching any skill. Examples are grace and courtesy of handling the chess pieces; social aspect of the game; practical life— polishing/dusting the pieces, setting up the environment; language, using the three-period-lesson to learn the names of the pieces; mastering the game by building up one difficulty at a time. It is based on the author's years of teaching chess to young children.

### *Please Help Me Do It Myself, Observation and Recordkeeping for the Primary and Elementary Class*

Montessori practice requires a scientist's ability to observe carefully, record observations, think, make an individual plan for each child, and act on this plan—and then continue to observe and adapt depending on the child's choices and mastery. At the 6-12 level the author shares how her students themselves mastered record keeping, planning, learning to make and meet goals (including local state/country requirements) and manage time. Additional primary class chapters: general knowledge book of the teacher; formal language book; beginning a new class; first six weeks in a continuing class; moving to a new environment; parent communication; human needs and tendencies; becoming a young adult.

### *The Joyful Child: Montessori, Global Wisdom for Birth to Three*

Five chapters with information and support for development in the first years of life; ten chapters on the development in the second two years. Also, preparing the environment; parenting and teaching; the Montessori approach to weaning; the Montessori 0-3 or Assistants to Infancy parent/teacher training.

This is the most translated book of this series and has brought Montessori to parents in many places.

### *The Music Environment for All Ages, Montessori Foundations for the Creative Personality*

A version of this information was joint published by AMI (Association Montessori Internationale) and NAMTA (North American Montessori Teachers Association) in the AMI Journal 2014-2015 issue: *The Montessori Foundations for the Creative Personality*. It gives parents and other educators an overview of the value and practice of music in the different stages of life: 0-3, 3-6, 6-12, 12-18, and even for the elderly.

### *The Red Corolla, Montessori Cosmic Education (for age 3-6+)*

Chapters include cosmic education; the work of the adult; the work of the child; culture from birth to age twelve; the music environment; and a Montessori glossary. There are universally tested cultural activities for this age: physics, botany, zoology, history, geography, art, music. In each area there is specific practical life work, sensorial exploration, lessons, sometimes artwork, and always the language that follows the experiences. All this information is based on lectures delivered in an AMI primary diploma course by the author.

## *The Universal Child, Guided by Nature*

(Part 1) Natural, inborn, human tendencies on which Montessori at all ages is based: movement, work, maximum effort, perfection, concentration, self-control, belonging, communication, and joy. (Part 2) Sharing Montessori in a variety of cultures. (Part 3) and the needs of adults whether they have, or have not, been met in the early formative years. (Part 4) How closeness to nature aids human development.

*Montessori for Family and Community*

Copyright © 2025 Susan Mayclin Stephenson
Michael Olaf Montessori Company
PO Box 1162
Arcata, CA 95518, USA
www.michaelolaf.net
michaelolafcompany@gmail.com
ISBN 978-1-879264-38-0

**Translation and foreign publishing rights**
contact: michaelolafbooks@gmail.com

**More Montessori Information**
https://susanart.net
www.montessori.edu
www.michaelolaf.net
https://susanmayclinstephenson.net

**Adult/child references**: Except in a few instances, to avoid confusion, "she" is used when referring to an adult and "he" when referring to a child.

**Reprint Permission**: Permission to share quotes from the book in newsletters, blogs, articles, university papers, books, book reviews, or via the Internet—is granted if it is being shared without payment, and if it includes a clear reference to the title, and the full name of the author.

**Gratitude for pictures and video clips**: I am very thankful to the parents and teachers from all over the world who have allowed me to record, through photos and video, children's stages of development in order to help others understand Montessori more deeply.

The video clips on our YouTube collection, "Montessori for family and community" can be accessed via the QR codes on the pages of this book and at the QR code below.

Please feel free to share them with anyone who will benefit.

Made in the USA
Middletown, DE
05 April 2025